Knowing the Love of Christ

KNOWING
THE
LOVE
OF
CHRIST

An Introduction to the Theology
of St. Thomas Aquinas

Michael Dauphinais
& Matthew Levering

UNIVERSITY OF NOTRE DAME PRESS
Notre Dame, Indiana

University of Notre Dame Press
Notre Dame, Indiana 46556
www.undpress.nd.edu

Published in the United States of America

Reprinted in 2011, 2014

Library of Congress Cataloging-in-Publication Data
Dauphinais, Michael, 1973–
Knowing the love of Christ : an introduction to the theology of St.
Thomas Aquinas / by Michael Dauphinais and Matthew Levering.
p.   cm.
Includes bibliographical references and index.
ISBN 0-268-03301-3 (cloth) — ISBN 0-268-03302-1 (paper)
1. Thomas, Aquinas, Saint, 1225?–1274.   2. Theology—History—
Middle Ages, 600–1500.   I. Levering, Matthew Webb, 1971–
II. Title.
BX4700.T6 D35   2002
230'.2'092—dc21
2002012610

∞ *This book is printed on acid-free paper.*

CONTENTS

ACKNOWLEDGMENTS

The fact that this book contains few footnotes makes it even more necessary for us to thank those who have made it possible for us to enter into the Thomistic tradition of theological enquiry. We have been blessed with so many wonderful teachers who have enriched our lives and enabled us to write this book. Not only those teachers to whom this book owes the largest debt, but also those with whom we have differed at significant points, have taught us much. We thus wish first to extend thanks and appreciation to our teachers at Duke, Notre Dame, and Boston College in whose courses we gained insight into Aquinas's way of thought: Stephen F. Brown, David Burrell, C.S.C., Romanus Cessario, O.P., Stanley Hauerwas, Thomas Hibbs, Mark Jordan, Matthew Lamb, Edward Mahoney, Thomas O'Meara, O.P., Jean Porter, Louis Roy, O.P., and Joseph Wawrykow. David Burrell and Romanus Cessario were readers for this book, and contributed greatly to the final product.

Other professors and colleagues have shaped our thinking about Aquinas in equally profound ways through their friendship and conversations. Here we wish to thank, among many others, John Boyle, Gilles Emery, O.P., Fred Freddoso, Paul Gondreau, John Goyette, Russell Hittinger, Michael Hoonhout, John Jenkins, C.S.C., Gregory LaNave, Carlo Leget, Steven Long, Ralph McInerny, Robert Miner, John O'Callaghan, Thomas Ryan, Michael Sherwin, O.P., Timothy Smith, David Solomon, and Christopher Thompson. We also owe a significant debt to the writings of Servais Pinckaers, O.P. and Jean-Pierre Torrell, O.P.

Our hope is that this book will enable many others to share in this wondrous pursuit of wisdom inspired by Aquinas and carried forward by these superb teachers. Of course, our ability to share in this academic community was fostered by other communities. We have received spiritual nourishment from our parishes, Christ the King and St. John the Baptist, and from Fr. Sylvester Ajagbe, Chaplain of Ave Maria College. Professor William Riordan, a great teacher, mentor, and friend, generously assigned a draft of this book to the students in his seminar on St. Thomas Aquinas, and we owe similar debts of gratitude to numerous other colleagues, students, and administrators at Ave Maria College. The associate director of the University of Notre Dame Press, Jeffrey Gainey, came up with the idea for the book and guided it every step of the way. He merits special thanks. We are also enormously appreciative of the work of Rebecca DeBoer, managing editor of the University of Notre Dame Press, whose corrections of the penultimate draft made this a much better book, and Margaret Gloster, art editor, who assisted us with the cover art for the book. Thomas Weinandy, O.F.M. Cap., offered an important correction at the proofs stage, which we gratefully incorporated.

Of the many blessings God has bestowed upon us, we are most grateful for our families. We must thank our wonderful parents, grandparents, in-laws, and extended families. Our children—Michael John, Thomas, and Joseph Dauphinais, and David, Andrew, and Irene Levering—give special meaning to everything we do. Lastly, our wives, Nancy Dauphinais and Joy Levering, read the entire manuscript in various drafts and encouraged our ongoing theological conversations. To Nancy and Joy, with great love, we dedicate this book.

Knowing the Love of Christ

INTRODUCTION

Just as an inexperienced mountain climber first apprentices to a master, and follows and develops the paths marked out by that master, so also it is with the theological ascent. When we enter into St. Thomas's spirit of humble contemplation of the divine mysteries, we will find him to be a true theological master. His theological masterpiece, the *Summa Theologiae,* is a series of questions. When we open the volumes of the *Summa,* we find three parts containing hundreds of questions divided into thousands of smaller questions ("articles"). Indeed, St. Thomas is like a child who, trusting in the teacher's knowledge, does not stop asking questions about God and all things in relation to God. Motivated by "faith seeking understanding," he continually strives for wisdom.

Before we begin our investigation of St. Thomas's theology, however, we might ask whether this striving after wisdom is appropriate for a follower of Jesus Christ. After all, in the Gospel of Luke, Jesus contrasts his disciples with the wise and learned of the world: "In that same hour he rejoiced in the Holy Spirit and said, 'I thank thee, Father, Lord of heaven and earth, that thou hast hidden these things from the wise and understanding and revealed them to babes; yea, Father, for such was thy gracious will'" (Lk 10:21). In the same Gospel, Jesus says, "Let the children come to me, and do not hinder them; for to such belongs the kingdom of God. Truly, I say to you, whoever does not receive the kingdom of God like a child shall not enter it" (Lk 18:16–17). St. Paul differentiates between the wisdom of the world and the gospel of the cross and resurrection of Jesus Christ: "Where is the wise man? Where is the scribe? Where is the debater of this age? Has not God made foolish the wisdom of the world? For since, in the wisdom of God, the world did not know God through wisdom, it pleased God through the folly of what we preach to save those who believe" (1 Cor 1:20–24).

Is St. Thomas the kind of "wise man" criticized by St. Paul as merely a "scribe" and a "debater of this age"? To come to understand St. Thomas, let us take a closer look at the passages from the Gospel of Luke. Both passages are immediately followed by emphasis on Jesus' role as *teacher*. After Jesus has praised God for revealing himself to "babes," an expert on the Mosaic Law "stood up to put him to the test, saying, 'Teacher, what shall I do to inherit eternal life?'" (Lk 10:25). The very same thing happens in the second passage. After Jesus has warned that entering the kingdom of God means becoming like a little child, immediately "a ruler asked him, 'Good teacher, what shall I do to inherit eternal life?'" (Lk 18:18). The experts and rulers turn to Jesus as teacher, but they expect to hear only human wisdom, what St. Paul calls the "wisdom of this world."

As St. Thomas recognizes, however, Jesus teaches a radically *new* kind of wisdom. Human wisdom investigates the relationships between all natural things. For example, a scientist is considered wise when he or she is able to demonstrate the links between all forms of life, from butterflies to supernovas. A ruler is considered wise when he or she is able to see how the most complex plans for the institutional organization of a society will affect the life of the ordinary citizen. Jesus' wisdom goes beyond merely human wisdom because Jesus reveals how God sees reality: it is the divine drama of redemption, in which God, out of unfathomable love, is calling us to perfect friendship with him. St. Thomas notes that theology is a coherent body of knowledge (a *scientia*) because its content comes from God's own knowledge. The teacher, God himself, is what is being taught.

This new wisdom *rearranges* all our previous untutored thoughts about God and the world. When through God's revelation in Jesus Christ we know the Trinity as Creator and Redeemer, we know ourselves in a new way, we know human history in a new way, we know human destiny in a new way. Everything is reordered. In learning who God is, we are also learning how God gives us what we need to attain our ultimate end or goal. God has called us to an end that exceeds our nature: participation in the trinitarian life. Theology therefore is about God and all things in relation to God "as their beginning and end" (*Summa Theologiae* part 1, question 1, article 7 [1, q.1., a.7]). This insight shapes the structure of the *Summa Theologiae,* which begins with the Trinity (God as our "beginning") and ends with eternal life in the Trinity (God as our "end"). The eight chapters of this book mirror the *Summa*'s structure. The book begins with a chapter on the triune God and then, in successive chapters, examines creation, the moral life (in two chapters), Jesus Christ, salvation, the Church and her sacraments, and eternal life. Each chapter refers the reader to key passages in the *Summa,* so the book should serve as a guide for further reading of the *Summa* itself.

St. Thomas's theology is rooted in Scripture and the Tradition of the Church, the two channels of God's revelation. Surprisingly, some theologians have criticized the *Summa Theologiae* as insufficiently biblical. In order to gain an accurate perspective, the present book will highlight St. Thomas's grounding in the narrative of Scripture as read and interpreted in the Church. St. Thomas explains that theology makes use of both philosophical insights and the teachings of the great theologians—especially those of the first six centuries after Christ—but only as *probable* arguments. By contrast, theology "properly uses the authority of the canonical Scriptures as an incontrovertible truth. . . . For our faith rests upon the revelation made to the apostles and prophets, who wrote the canonical books" (1, q.1, a.8, ad 2 [reply to objection 2]). The Bible, as canonized and read in the Church, contains Christ's words and deeds as the Holy Spirit willed for them to be recorded. His words and deeds are prepared for and prefigured in the Old Testament and manifested fully in the New Testament, which itself prefigures our final union with the Trinity in glory.

Yet if the Scriptures, as read and interpreted in the Church, have opened up Jesus' wisdom to St. Thomas, are we saying that the *Summa Theologiae* is the final word? The novelist Walker Percy once warned against exaggerating the scope of any human worldview by referring to a story from the Danish philosopher Søren Kierkegaard. Kierkegaard described a person who "read [the philosopher] Hegel, understood himself and the universe perfectly by noon, but then had the problem of living out the rest of the day."[1] Does St. Thomas's theology fall into this trap of claiming to have understood everything perfectly, so that the reader of this book will have nothing else to discover?

---

1. Walker Percy, *Signposts in a Strange Land,* ed. Patrick Samway (New York: Farrar, Straus and Giroux, 1991), 375.

On the contrary. Following the path of St. Thomas's *Summa,* this book will move from divine beatitude—God's own unfathomable happiness—to our future heavenly beatitude, our sharing in God's unfathomable happiness. St. Thomas's work is not a closed system. It is sensitive at all points to the inexhaustible *mystery* of the Trinity and the divine plan. God's wisdom and self-giving love, which we imitate by following Jesus Christ, are always ever-greater than we can imagine. On the mystery of the divine love, St. Thomas writes, "A lover is placed outside himself, and made to pass into the object of his love" (1, q.20, a.2, ad 1). Or as St. Thomas put it near the end of his life, during which he was experiencing spiritual ecstasies: "I cannot do any more. Everything I have written seems to me as straw in comparison with what I have seen."[2] His work, as he says in the *Summa's* prologue, is for beginners in the quest for wisdom; it ends in the supreme personal vision of the divine wisdom and love.

If one temptation is to exaggerate the comprehensiveness of St. Thomas's theology, however, the other temptation is to undervalue what he has achieved. It might seem that by calling his writings "straw," he was renouncing his labors as worthless. This is far from the case. His contemplation of Christ as "the way, the truth, and the life" united him more and more perfectly to Christ, until at the end of his life he entered so fully into contemplation that he could write no longer. God inspired him to teach us in a final way: after teaching through his extraordinary writings, in the end he taught also what the true goal of these writings is, namely, union with God. This goal hardly negates the study and teaching that have gone before, but rather is their wondrous fulfillment.

What Walker Percy and Kierkegaard call the "problem of living out the rest of the day," then, is not the result of having understood everything in the morning—having understood everything, that is, but how to live. Instead, if we follow St. Thomas's contemplative path, it is the problem of truly entering into (intellectually and morally) the mysteries to which we are united by faith, hope, and charity, aided by prayer and the sacraments. Although we stumble and fall often on this journey, no other journey can satisfy our hearts' yearning for the inexhaustible wisdom and love that never end. As a spiritual master, St. Thomas's entire theology is geared toward our coming, as adopted sons and daughters, to rest in and *enjoy*

---

2. Jean-Pierre Torrell, O.P., *St. Thomas Aquinas,* vol. 1: *The Person and His Work,* trans. Robert Royal (Washington, D.C.: Catholic University of America Press), 1996), 289.

the divine Persons by being made partakers "of the divine Word and of the Love proceeding, so as freely to know God truly and to love God rightly" (1, q.38, a.1). His is a theology of divine gift.

The chapters of this book are therefore best described as an invitation to enter into the Church's ongoing conversation about the meaning of the gospel, a conversation which St. Thomas himself entered, and which, guided by him, we now enter. This conversation—whose goal is the vision of the Father, in the Son, through the Holy Spirit—is not only a conversation through the generations with other human beings, but also, and indeed primarily, a conversation with Christ our teacher.

CHAPTER ONE

THE TRIUNE GOD

In Eastern Rite liturgies, before the reading of Scripture, the priest proclaims, "Wisdom! Be attentive." The proper hearing of Scripture requires a contemplative attitude, a burning desire to know the Wisdom of God. St. Thomas traces this contemplative fire back to the inspired authors of Scripture itself. In the prologue to his *Commentary on John,* he argues that it was the grace of intense conversation with God, rooted in love, that enabled men such as Isaiah and St. John to express in human words the truth of God's Word. As St. Gregory of Nyssa says in his classic treatment of contemplation, *The Life of Moses,* "The knowledge of God is a mountain steep indeed and difficult to climb—the majority of people scarcely reach its base. If one were a Moses, he would ascend higher and hear the sound of trumpets which, as the text of the history says, becomes louder as one advances. For the preaching of the divine nature is truly a trumpet blast, which strikes the hearing, being already loud at the beginning but becoming yet louder at the end."[1] The higher we ascend toward the mysteries of the triune God, the more glorious and harmonious will the "notes" of Christian revelation sound in our ears.

The Contemplative Approach

This contemplative movement of ascent is inspired by the triune God's "descent" in revealing himself through the missions

---

1. St. Gregory of Nyssa, *The Life of Moses,* trans. Abraham J. Malherbe and Everett Ferguson (New York: Paulist Press, 1978), 93.

of the Son and Holy Spirit in human history. Inspired by the incarnate Son, Jesus Christ, and the Holy Spirit, we are able to appreciate the contemplative path up the mountain toward the triune God that St. Thomas charts for us. This path begins with contemplation of God in his oneness. The contemplative ascent first investigates what belongs to God's oneness so that the discussion of God as Trinity does not fall into tri-theism. The wonder of God is that in him three is one, and one is three. This truth acts like dynamite upon our limited notions of God.

Though many amateurs attempt mountain climbing, few undertake the most daring climb of all, the mountain of contemplative knowledge of God. Savoring the difficulty and thrill of the climb, let us follow St. Thomas on his ascent.

God Revealed to Moses

All theological insights into God's oneness flow from contemplation of the way in which God revealed his name to Moses. Having attracted Moses' attention by the miracle of a bush that burned without being consumed, God named himself "I am who I am," "He who is," or YHWH (Ex 3:14–16). The Jewish biblical scholar Nahum Sarna has this to say about God's name in the context of the function of names in ancient Israel:

> The name is intended to connote character and nature, the totality of the intricate, interwoven, manifold forces that make up the whole personality of the bearer of the name. In the present case, therefore, God's reply to Moses means that the Tetragrammaton (YHWH) expresses the quality of Being. However, it is not Being as opposed to nonbeing, not Being as an abstract philosophical notion, but Being in the sense of the reality of God's active, dynamic Presence.[2]

The name "I am who I am" identifies the God who reveals himself through the miracle of the burning bush as a fire that never diminishes because its fuel is never consumed. Consider the difference between this fire and

---

2. Nahum M. Sarna, *Exploring Exodus: The Origins of Biblical Israel* (New York: Schocken Books, 1996), 52.

other kinds of fire we know. The sun will burn for billions of years, but it will eventually burn out. Even now, its fuel is being consumed. Our lives, too, are like fires. Like a candle, our lives burn quickly or slowly, and sooner or later the wick will be consumed. In contrast, the miracle of the burning bush suggests that God, like the sun or like ourselves, is in act (aflame with energy) but that, unlike the sun, his act (energy) is always fully present, never diminished. The divine Act is infinite, unchanging Presence. Let us see what this means.

Finite Existence Depends upon Infinite Existence

In light of this revelation to Moses, St. Thomas seeks to contemplate God's name "He who is." Consider everything that exists in a finite (limited) way: a star, a bird, a memory, and so forth. All of these things exist, but none had to be. Existing and "existing as star" are not the same. "To be" does not mean "to be *star.*" If it did, everything that existed would have to be star. This distinction is that between existence and essence. Existence answers the question "is it?" Essence answers the question "what is it?"

Only a reality whose essence *is existence,* whose nature is simply Act, exists necessarily and in an unlimited, perfectly full, infinite mode. Everything else—a star, a bird, a memory—need not have existed and, once in existence, need not continue to exist in the same way. Such things do not exist in an unlimited or infinite mode. Rather, since "to be" does not mean "to be *star,*" a star possesses a finite and limited mode of existence.

St. Thomas shows that the existence of finite things—contingent beings such as stars, birds, humans, and so forth—depends upon the existence of infinite Act. Since a finite thing does not exist by its nature, every finite thing must be brought into existence. Consider the case of a human being. Before Jane is conceived, there was a *possibility* that a human being named Jane would come into existence. It was always possible that a human being would be born who would have the particular existence that Jane does. However, it took the procreative act of Jane's parents to make that possibility *actual.* No finite thing can explain its own existence without reference to something that *caused* a movement from possible to actual existence. If Jane could trace her ancestry all the way back to the Big Bang, would that then explain her existence?

The answer is no. In any historical chain of finite causes, there remains the fact that existence is not a necessary attribute of any finite thing. For each finite thing, the question is ultimately, where does existence per se come from? Why, here and now, is there something rather than nothing? Every finite reality, at every moment, depends upon something else for existence. The original explosion is itself a finite mode of existence. Since the nature of "to be" is not "to be Big Bang," the original explosion itself must have been a mere possibility. It did not have to occur. Its existence, too, must be explained by reference to something that caused a movement from possible to actual existence.

St. Thomas points out that if one had an infinite chain of finite things being moved from potentiality to actuality, and in turn moving other finite things from potentiality to actuality, what would explain the existence of the infinite chain of finite things? Just as each finite thing cannot in itself account for its existence, but instead must be "actualized" by a prior being, the same would hold for the infinite chain of finite things. The existence of the chain itself depends upon a movement from possibility to actuality caused by a being that does not receive its existence from anything else. In order to explain the existence of the chain of finite things, there must be a cause that is itself uncaused. In other words, there must be a cause which has existence not merely possibly, but by definition—a cause which is infinite actuality, infinite "to be." This cause is "He who is," infinite Act.

St. Thomas suggests other ways to identify "He who is." For example, we find complexity and order in irrational things, which, lacking rational capabilities, could not have placed that order within themselves. From the pattern of a snowflake to the motions of the galaxies, examples of "the laws of nature" abound. These laws could not come from "nature" itself. "Nature" is not a rational being who could institute order in a complex system. Something must have given order to nature—and this orderer is "He who is," because only God transcends the realm of "nature" and thus could give it an order.

Similarly, we find degrees of existence in the universe. The rock exists, but it does not exist as fully as the plant, which is alive. A worm exists more abundantly than a plant, since the worm not only is alive, but can move itself. A dolphin exists more abundantly than a worm, since dolphins have complex structures of communication. The existence of a human being is of a higher degree than that of a dolphin, because human beings have the power of knowing universal truths and loving them as good. Degrees of perfection in being indicate a *standard* of perfection in being, by which one thing is measured as existing more or less fully.

Although God is not proportional to finite beings (because God is infinite), this standard of perfection that gives measure to all things is infinite Act, "He who is."

Our Knowledge of God

A contemplative—one who, moved by love, has savored the sheer wonder of existing—will experience the joy and awe contained in the statement "God is infinite existence." This statement does not reduce the mystery of the divine. God is incomprehensible. God infinitely surpasses any human concept of him. Our finite minds cannot even come close to grasping the infinite mode of being that is God. We can know what God is *not,* but we cannot know—in the sense of fully comprehending—what God *is.* Finite existence cannot comprehend infinite existence.

This includes even our knowledge of God by divine revelation in Jesus Christ. St. Thomas, nevertheless, argues that we do possess a greater knowledge of God through the revelation of grace than we could have by natural reason alone. We do know God more fully since he manifests more of his actions to us and he teaches us truths unattainable by natural reason, preeminently, that God is three and one. For instance, the knowledge that God justifies sinners through the passion (cross) of Christ makes known to us God's great love and mercy.

Revealed knowledge does not overturn the normal structure of the way human beings attain knowledge through our senses. Revelation offers new sensible realities, such as the revelation of the Trinity at Jesus' baptism, along with a greater intellectual light with which to perceive these realities, namely, the light of grace (1, q.12, a.13). The normal structure of human knowing remains the same: by an intellectual light, we perceive sensible realities. Revelation offers grace, which illumines our minds to perceive the meaning of the sensible realities of God's marvelous deeds.

There exists a paradox or a dynamic tension at the heart of the revelation of God in Christ. On the one hand, God has revealed himself to us for our salvation in a way that far exceeds anything we could construct from our knowledge of the world. On the other hand, our knowledge of God's revelation remains subject to the usual way we know things of this world. The dynamic tension exists in the New Testament. 1 John 1:1 depicts the concrete character of our knowledge of God in Christ: "That which was from the beginning, which we have heard, which we have seen with our eyes, which we have looked upon and touched with our hands, concerning the word of life"; whereas 1 Corinthians 13:12 reveals the profound limits of our present knowledge: "For now we see in a mirror dimly, but then face to face. Now I know in part; then I shall understand fully, even as I have been fully understood." St. Thomas and Scripture consistently hold together knowing and unknowing.

If God transcends any words and concepts we derive from the world, how can we speak truly about God? As St. Augustine noted at the beginning of his *Confessions,* our language is inadequate to capture the majesty of God, but God himself has commanded that we praise him with our language. Language about God has an analogous character. St. Thomas considers analogous names with respect to a "prime analogate" (focal meaning) that serves as the standard for the proper application of the word in other cases. The various meanings are proportioned toward the focal meaning. Consider the word "healthy." When used in the two phrases "a healthy dinner" and "a healthy Daniel," it is used analogously. The word "healthy" here has two different meanings, but they are ordered to one focal meaning. We thus call a vegetarian dinner "healthy" though the focal meaning for healthy is the well-functioning human body. The vegetables in the dinner would be better described as "dead" than as "healthy." What is signified is the perfection of health, but the manner of signifying is different with respect to a "healthy dinner" and a "healthy Daniel."

By drawing on the structure of analogous words, St. Thomas shows how we can speak meaningfully of God's perfections while maintaining that God *is* his perfections in a way unlike the way creatures *possess* their perfections. God is wise in a way wholly other than the way Socrates is wise. We can say of Socrates that he becomes wise, but we cannot say the same of God, for this would indicate that God is something distinct from his wisdom. We can understand God by means of various concepts, such as goodness, wisdom, and love, even while we understand that God is simple and one. This way of expressing our understanding of God shows both the inadequacy of affirmations about God and the appropriateness of making such affirmations. For example, when Scripture reveals that "God is love" (1 Jn 4:8), we must be cautious of identifying God with our preconceived notions of love. Moreover, even when we attempt to let the narrative of Scripture shape our concept of love, we know that our concept is never fully adequate to the perfection of God as it exists between the Father, Son, and Holy Spirit.

God's Simplicity

Although we describe God by a diversity of names, God's essence is not diverse, but rather is simple. God's simplicity has two implications. First, God is not in any way a "composite." By contrast, creatures are composites of possibility and actuality, of matter and form, and of various attributes or characteristics. Since, as we have seen, God is sheer Act, there is no "possibility" or untapped potential in God that could be brought into "actuality." God is already and eternally the infinite fullness of being, the fullness of actuality. God thus cannot be material or bodily. Everything material is a finite or limited form of existence, and thus is composed of possibility and actuality. God is pure spirit (cf. Jn 4:24). Moreover, God's knowledge is God himself, God's will is God himself, God's mercy is God himself, and so forth. The attributes are distinct in our mode of thinking, but they are one in God. Consider that Jane's intelligence is distinct from Jane herself. She is not her mind. She is a body-soul *composite* with various powers and faculties. On the other hand, God *is* any attribute that God possesses. Since God is sheer Act, there is no composition or potential for change in God. God is infinite, undivided Act.

Second, God's "simplicity" means that God is not "a being" among the varieties of beings. Just as there is no proportion between infinite and finite, there is no proportion between infinite existence and finite existence. God cannot be a limited being among other beings. God is fully present everywhere and in all things not materially or spatially, but by sustaining finite existence in his eternal "now," his active Presence. God, infinitely active, is unchanging in the sense that nothing can be added to or taken away from the perfectly full, glorious divine Act who is "He who is." As God taught through the prophet Malachi, "For I the Lord do not change; therefore you, O sons of Jacob, are not consumed" (Mal 3:6). The vibrant fullness of divine Act sustains the existence of all human beings and sustains the covenants he has established with Israel and, ultimately, the New Covenant in Jesus Christ.

God's Perfection

All perfections are perfections of *being*. Possessing a perfection means that one exists more perfectly, whereas possessing a defect means that one exists in a deficient or constrained way. Creatures are perfected when they become the fullness of what they can be—when their natural powers are fully *in act*. A tulip attains its perfection when it is a mature flower: its potencies have been fully actualized. A mature tulip is in potential to be corrupted, to exist in a lesser way. Thus a tulip lacks its proper existence, or exists in a defective way, when people trample on it and cause its stem to break. A human being is perfected when he or she attains not only bodily maturity, but also the full range of rational powers. Jane's mind is perfected insofar as she knows truth and embraces the truth in love. Her mind is more *in act* the more it apprehends the causes of things.

In St. Thomas's words, "a thing is perfect in proportion to its state of actuality, because we call that perfect which lacks nothing of the mode of its perfection" (1, q.4, a.1). Since God is infinite Act, God is perfect. No further perfection can be added to God, since nothing can be added to the fullness of unlimited being. Every perfection of existence belongs supremely to God. God possesses no defects, since a defect implies a lack in existence—the very opposite of God's unlimited Act. As the Psalmist wrote, "This God—his way is perfect" (Ps 18:30).

God's Knowledge

When we meet a wise person, we are impressed. At the end of the book of Ecclesiastes, an admirer of Ecclesiastes praised him: "Besides being wise, the Preacher also taught the people knowledge, weighing and studying and arranging proverbs with great care. The preacher sought to find pleasing words, and uprightly he wrote words of truth" (Eccles 12:9–10). Our minds are made to know truth, not simply to seek it. Knowledge perfects our being, since our being is *rational* being. Acquiring knowledge, however, is a laborious process for us. We must slowly reason our way to truth. The admirer of Ecclesiastes thus adds, "Of making many books there is no end, and much study is a weariness of the flesh" (Eccles 12:12). Nonetheless, arriving at truth is delightful. When we learn why things are the way they are, we experience the joy of one who emerges from darkness into daylight. Compared to the vastness of the cosmos, human beings are infinitesimal; yet by making judgments of truth the human mind can draw into itself the cosmos and even attain a limited knowing of the Creator.

If we can come to possess knowledge according to our finite mode of existence, God possesses knowledge according to his infinite mode of existence. St. Paul rejoices in "the depth of the riches and wisdom and knowledge of God!" (Rom 11:33). St. Thomas notes that knowledge is connected with immateriality or spiritual nature (1, q.14, a.1). If, in order to know a cow, we had to fit the actual cow into our head, we would never know much. Similarly, if our reasoning were unable to move beyond what our senses could record through memory and imagination, we would not be able to reason to a judgment of truth. Since our mind is not matter, but rather is spirit (the brain is the mind's instrument), we can form concepts of other things, and can judge these concepts to be true or false.

God, as pure Act, is supremely immaterial (pure spirit), and therefore God supremely knows. He does not acquire knowledge, nor does he reason by a process of discovery. Rather, the truth of all things is in God. Since God is simple, God's knowledge is the same as his Act, his being. His understanding and what he understands are the same. In his one simple, eternal Act, he knows himself through himself. Furthermore, in knowing his infinite being, he knows all the finite ways in which his infinite being could be shared and all the ways in which finite existence could suffer corruption. As Jesus reassures his disciples, "Are not five sparrows sold for two pennies? And not one of them is forgotten before God. Why, even the hairs of your head are all numbered. Fear not; you are of more value than many sparrows" (Lk 12:6–7).

God's Will

"Will" describes the rational appetite, the dynamism whereby the mind desires as good the truth that it knows, and rests in or delights in this truth. God, in knowing himself, rests in himself as good. God therefore possesses both knowledge and will, both of which are his one simple Act. The movement of the will tending toward the good is *love*. St. Thomas explains that love is "the unitive force" because love is when we will for ourselves union with the good that we know. Love can be called a unitive force even in God, although the good that he wills for himself is himself. Love is also unitive because in willing good for another, we put the other in place of ourselves. In other words, love is self-giving.

In embracing the truth in love, therefore, we will to share the good with others. In loving himself as good, God freely wills to share himself,

to share his being. Created being is nothing other than a finite participation, or sharing, in God's infinite being. Literally, then, God loves all
finite things *into existence* by giving them a finite participation in his infinite Act. In so doing, God is willing the divine goodness, since finite being
is a sharing in the divine goodness. Just as God knows all else by knowing his own being, so also God wills all else by willing his own goodness.
As St. Thomas says, "God's love infuses and creates goodness" (1, q.20,
a.2). In loving us, God loves his own gift. The more we possess the fullness of being, the more God loves us; but our being is always his gift.

Since the goodness of God is perfect, he lacks nothing. God's life,
his eternal Presence, is perfect beatitude or happiness. He does not *need*
creatures. God's creative will therefore is utterly free. He gives us existence
by an unimaginably free gift of pure love. In knowing himself and embracing the goodness that he knows, God knows all the finite ways that his
infinite existence might be shared, and he freely wills that some of these
finite ways come into existence as rocks, tulips, cows, humans, angels, and
so forth. Thus we speak of God's free creation of the universe.

As the good Creator, God is just and merciful. St. Thomas notes that
"the order of the universe, which is seen both in effects of nature and in
effects of will [the free will of rational creatures], shows forth the justice
of God" (1, q.21, a.1). The goodness of God's wisdom and will is manifested when he gives each thing its due, although creatures owe a debt to
God rather than the other way around. God is merciful in that he gives
creatures far more than their due; in a certain sense, all is mercy. Mercy
does not go against justice, however, but rather goes beyond justice by
bestowing an undeserved gift. In every act of God toward creatures, therefore, we find both justice and mercy. God does all things justly, in accor-
dance with his wisdom and goodness. Yet everything that God does is also
an act of mercy, since God gives to creatures far more than is proportion-
ate to their deserving. In showing us how to become like God, Jesus ties
justice and mercy together: "Blessed are those who hunger and thirst for
righteousness, for they shall be satisfied. Blessed are the merciful, for they
shall obtain mercy" (Mt 5:6–7).

The Trinity

Knowledge of the Trinity comes from God's self-revelation in Jesus Christ.
At many points in the Gospels, Jesus teaches that he is the "I am" revealed

to Moses. He is fully human, and yet he is fully divine. The Gospel of John is filled with such clues that Jesus is God made flesh. For instance Jesus says, "Before Abraham was, I am" (Jn 8:58). The other Gospels also describe Jesus claiming the divine name. Consider the time when the disciples, fearing they would capsize and drown in the sea, catch sight of Jesus walking toward them on the water. Imagining that they are seeing a ghost, they are paralyzed by terror. Jesus' words of reassurance should be translated, "Take heart, I am (*ego eimi*); do not be afraid" (Mt 14:27). He is the "I am" who is revealing his divinity by his miraculous power over the chaos of sea and storm. It is only this "I am" who could truly calm the storm experienced personally and collectively by sinners. After his resurrection, Jesus in the Gospel of Matthew commissions his disciples: "Go therefore and make disciples of all nations, baptizing them in the name of the Father and of the Son and of the Holy Spirit, teaching them to observe all that I have commanded you; and lo, I am with you always, to the close of the age" (Mt 28:19–20). Jesus reveals that God is a Trinity of Persons.

The one God is Father, Son, and Holy Spirit. How is such a God still one? If one, how three? How can the three Persons exist without undermining divine simplicity? The guideposts for our ascent will now be recognized only by faith, since only by becoming spiritual children in Christ can we know this mystery. As we reflect upon the mystery of the Trinity, the weakness of our human intellect means that we have reached heights conditioned by low oxygen and low visibility. The goal of our ascent—the inexhaustibly glorious vista that we seek—is the trinitarian identity of "He who is."

St. John and St. Paul on the Trinity

St. Thomas attributes the trinitarian profundity of the Gospel of John to the traditional identification of St. John with the "beloved disciple" described in John's Gospel: "because secrets are revealed to friends . . . Jesus confided his secrets in a special way to that disciple who was specially loved. . . . it is John who sees the light of the Incarnate Word more excellently and expresses it to us" (*Commentary on John*, prologue). The other evangelists focus more upon the humanity of Christ, while John, because of his contemplative friendship with Christ, "flies like an eagle above the cloud of human weakness and looks upon the light of unchanging truth with the most lofty and firm eyes of the heart. . . . gazing on the very deity of our Lord Jesus Christ, by which he is equal to the Father" (ibid.). St. John was inspired to give the Son of God the name Word: "In the beginning was the Word, and the Word was with God, and the Word was God" (Jn 1:1). This verse teaches us that the Word is distinct from the God the Father, and yet the Word is fully God. It also indicates that there is an internal procession in God, since a "word" or concept *proceeds from* the mind. Similarly, John names the Holy Spirit *Paraclete,* meaning advocate, counselor, or comforter who brings us into the fullness of the Word.

John also suggests the way in which the temporal missions of the Son and the Holy Spirit are related to their eternal processions in God. The temporal missions describe the Son and the Holy Spirit as sent by the Father *into the world;* the eternal processions refer to the Son and the Holy Spirit as coming forth from the Father *within the Godhead.* Jesus, speaking of his divine Sonship, testifies to his own procession from the Father: "I proceeded and came forth from God; I came not of my own accord, but he sent me" (Jn 8:42), and "He who believes in me, believes not in me but in him who sent me" (Jn 12:44). Jesus also speaks of the Holy Spirit's procession: "But when the Counselor [Holy Spirit] comes, whom I shall send to you from the Father, even the Spirit of truth, who proceeds from the Father, he will bear witness to me" (Jn 15:26; cf. 16:7). The procession of the Holy Spirit is thus from the Father through the Son.

In addition to St. John's insights, the teaching of St. Paul has taken on special importance in trinitarian doctrine. St. Paul describes the temporal mission or sending of the Son: "For God has done what the law, weakened by the flesh, could not do: sending his own Son in the likeness of sinful flesh" (Rom 8:3). He names the Son "the image of the invisible God" (Col 1:15). The name "image" fits well with St. John's use of "Word." St. Paul also describes the procession of the Holy Spirit as a gift of love: "God's love has been poured into our hearts through the Holy Spirit which has been given to us" (Rom 5:5).

Processions in God

St. Thomas begins with this biblical revelation and seeks to understand it more deeply. As we have seen, there are two processions in God, that of the Son and that of the Holy Spirit. To understand these processions, St. Thomas employs analogies from processions in creatures. One analogy that he uses is that of Adam, Eve, and Abel (1, q.36, a.3, ad 1). Like the great Eastern theologians, such as St. Gregory of Nazianzus, he uses this familial analogy—the procession (coming forth) of a child from a father and mother—to illumine how the Holy Spirit proceeds immediately from the Father and mediately from the Son.[3] In St. Thomas's words, however, this analogy is ultimately "inept," although hardly useless, because it relies upon a bodily image. St. Gregory of Nazianzus weighed other analogies for the trinitarian processions: source (Father), fountain (Son), river (Holy Spirit); and sun, ray, light. He found both to be ultimately inadequate since they are physical processions.[4]

Since God is not bodily, there cannot be material processions in God, as when a distinct bodily substance comes forth from a source. The divine processions must be immaterial and remain within God. Therefore an analogy from spiritual substance, namely the human mind, is necessary. Our rational powers of intellect and will are what differentiate us from other animals and make us uniquely in the image of God. St. Gregory of Nyssa identified, without fully developing, an analogy from the human mind: "As in our own case we say that the word is from the mind, and no more entirely the same as the mind, than altogether other than it . . . , in like manner, too, the Word of God by its self-subsistence is distinct from Him from whom it has its subsistence."[5] In *On the Trinity*, St. Augustine discussed numerous analogies and developed the two trinitarian analogies that St. Thomas employs most centrally: lover (Father), beloved (Son), love (Holy Spirit); and mind, intellect, will.

St. Thomas uses the former analogy when describing the relation of the Holy Spirit to the Father and the Son (1, q.37). He uses the latter analogy when offering a sketch of the trinitarian processions (1, q.27). The latter analogy—mind, intellect, will—is appropriate especially because it reveals the profound significance of St. John's theology of the divine Word.

---

3. St. Gregory of Nazianzus, *The Fifth Theological Oration: On the Holy Spirit*, trans. Charles Gordon Brown and James Edward Swallow, in *Nicene and Post-Nicene Fathers*, vol. 7: *Cyril of Jerusalem, Gregory Nazianzen* (Peabody, Mass.: Hendrickson, 1994 [1894]), no. 11 (p. 321).

4. Ibid., nos. 31–33 (p. 328).

5. St. Gregory of Nyssa, *The Great Catechism*, trans. William Moore and Henry Austin Wilson, in *Nicene and Post-Nicene Fathers*, vol. 5: *Gregory of Nyssa* (Peabody, Mass.: Hendrickson, 1994 [1893]), chap. 1 (p. 476).

The human mind is spirit, not physical matter, although it operates through the brain as its instrument. The mind or soul possesses spiritual powers of intellect and will. In the intellect's act of knowing, a concept is formed. For example, when we see something with four legs and hear the sound "moo," our minds generate the concept "cow." The concept "cow" does not exist independently in the sense that the mind knows the concept, which reflects the actually existing cow. This would trap our knowledge inside of our heads. Instead, the mind knows the actually existing cow *by means of* the concept "cow." This concept can be called an inner word. The concept (inner word) proceeds from the mind. Understanding "cow" as part of God's creation, the will embraces what is known—"cow"—as good. The cow may exude unpleasant odors and may not be welcome in our living rooms. Nevertheless, provided there is sufficient outdoor green pasture, we can say that it is better that a cow exist than not exist. This embrace of the goodness of the cow is the procession of love.

Within the mind, therefore, there are two processions: the procession of the word (concept, image) and the procession of love. These processions are distinct, yet the mind remains perfectly one. The processions of intellect and will in the mind thus provide an *analogy* for the biblically revealed trinitarian processions of the Son and Holy Spirit from the Father.

Relations in God

The analogy limps, however, not only because of our example of the cow, but because the mind remains really one. The dual processions of knowing and loving from the mind do not indicate that they exist distinctly from the mind. Why, then, are the divine processions not like the human mind's processions, in which knowing and loving certainly are distinct, but the mind is really just one, not three? Are the processions of Word and Love sufficient to ground a true distinction of Persons in the one God? St. Thomas answers this question by examining the *relations* that arise in the divine processions of Son and Holy Spirit from the Father. The category of "relation" is required to understand the tripersonal God who reveals himself by the relational and dynamic name of Father, Son, and Holy Spirit. We should keep in mind throughout that the Persons are best understood as relations because they are more like verbs than nouns.

There are not divine Persons who then relate; rather, the Persons are the relating. Let us therefore examine "relation."

Examples of relations include teacher-student and boss-employee. For our purposes, it is helpful to consider the example of fatherhood. Before conceiving a child, a man is simply a man, not a "father." Afterwards, however, the man is a "father." The man has been changed. He exists now in a new relational way, as father of a child. This is why many parents comment that the adjustment to the first child is more earth-shaking than the second, third, or sixth. The first child moves the parents into a new state of relational being. The same new relational existence is also in the child, who exists relationally as child of the father.

The divine processions mean that there are "relations" in God. The Father generates the Son. The Son is related as offspring to the Father; the Father is related as source to the Son. In fact, the Father is the relation "fatherhood" and the Son is the relation "sonship." The Father could not be the Father without the Son; the Son could not be the Son without the Father. East and west can also be relational descriptions. If a tree is planted to the west of a house, then the house is to the east of the tree. This example differs from the relations of origin in the Trinity, however, because the tree could easily have been planted on the other side of the house. The relations of Father and Son are such that they could not be reversed. Even in human terms, my father and I cannot switch places without destroying our identities as father and son.

analogy of east + west (handwritten margin note)

The procession of the Holy Spirit is called "love" or "love proceeding." The Father, through the Son, breathes forth the Holy Spirit as love. The source of the Holy Spirit in the Father and Son is called "spiration," and the Spirit's coming forth is called "procession." As Jesus says, "when the Counselor [Holy Spirit] comes, whom I shall send to you from the Father, even the Spirit of truth, who proceeds from the Father, he will bear witness to me" (Jn 15:26).

Do orthodox believe this? (handwritten margin note)

The Holy Spirit is related to the Father and Son as "love proceeding"; the Father and Son are related to the Holy Spirit as principle or source. In breathing forth the Spirit, the Father and the Son act as *one* principle or source because nothing distinguishes the Son from the Father other than the Father-Son relation. The Holy Spirit, as love proceeding, is a relation distinct from the Father and Son. The Holy Spirit subsists or exists distinctly in God because "love proceeding" differs from "Fathering" and "Sonship." Thus the Holy Spirit is the third Person of the Trinity.

Although the Father and the Son are the source of the Holy Spirit, this relation in the Father and the Son does not form a fourth Person in the Trinity. In God, the Father is *Father* in breathing forth the Holy Spirit; the Son is *Son* in breathing forth the Holy Spirit. The breathing forth of the Holy Spirit does not cause Father to be something other than Father, or Son something other than Son. Therefore "spirator" is the same as "Father" and the same as "Son." Spiration does not constitute a fourth relation that exists on its own in God. Rather than being a distinct mode of existence in God, spiration is the same as Father and Son, whereas the love spirated is the Holy Spirit.

[handwritten margin note: Father + Son have 2 relations]

The Divine Persons

We have identified three distinct relations or modes of existing within God: fatherhood, sonship, love proceeding. Unlike in creatures, however, whatever is in God, is God. There is no composition in God, who is pure Act. The distinct relations in God are not three modes in which a "one God" appears (the heresy of Sabellius). Each distinct relation is fully God, fully "He who is." Each distinct relation is therefore a divine Person, a distinct subject. Does this mean that God is not really one, but that there are three gods?

Since God is simple, whatever is in God must be God. Each distinct relation in God must *be* God. Yet the category of relation has two aspects: relation *to* and relation *in*. The relation always exists in something, and the relation is always to another thing. Relation *to* gives us insight into how the relations in God are distinct: the Persons are distinct solely in relation (of origin) *to* each other. Relation *in* gives us insight into how the relations in God are each fully God, and how together they are fully God. Thus each Person is a distinct way of existing (subsisting) *in* "He who is," the simple divine Act. Since each divine Person is sheer subsisting relation, the Persons should be thought of not as static nouns, but as active verbs: the one divine Act is in act in three distinct relatings, or "Persons."

As regards relatings-*to*, the divine relations are perfectly distinct Persons. Thus, referring to the Father as the eternal source of the Godhead, Jesus teaches, "The Father is greater than I" (Jn 14:28; cf. *Commentary on John,* chap. 14, lecture 8). As regards relatings-*in*, each divine Person (and the three together) *is* the divine being. Jesus teaches, "I and the Father are one" (Jn 10:30). God the Trinity is three Persons subsisting distinctly in relation *to* each other *in* the divine being.

Since the divine Persons are distinguished only by relation to each other, the divine being is not threefold. Although the divine being is the same as the divine Persons—the one God is the Trinity—the human mind requires different concepts to express the different aspects of the reality of God. St. Thomas leads us away from imagining that the divine Persons "emerge" from the essence (the divine being) or, in their mutual harmonious relations, *bring about* the unity that we call the essence or being. Rather, "being" here expresses the mystery of divine unity. "He who is" and "Father, Son, and Holy Spirit" are therefore complementary names.

Naming the Persons

St. Thomas begins with the inspired New Testament names—Father, Son, Word, image, Holy Spirit, gift, love—and the New Testament's references to the processions of the Son and the Holy Spirit. As we have seen, it would be a grave mistake to think of the Word as the "part" of God who knows, or the Holy Spirit as the "part" of God who loves. God is perfect knowing and loving. Similarly, it is not true that only the Father creates, or that only the Son redeems, or that only the Spirit sanctifies; these are all acts of the triune God.

What then is unique, within the Trinity, to the Father, or to the Son, or to the Holy Spirit? This final contemplative step requires recognizing the beauty of the *order* of the trinitarian processions—an order of eternal processions, not an order in time. What is so exciting and beautiful about an order?

Father, Son, and Holy Spirit subsist in one being, so each Person has equality with and *indwells* the others in a perfect dynamic communion of self-giving wisdom and love. This perfect communion of the distinct Persons in the one God is the source of endless contemplation. To appreciate the perfect communion, we must grasp what makes each Person distinct from the others. The Father is the unbegotten, uncaused source of everything. What could be more unique and incommunicably personal than being the source of all? In the mystery of the Father we have the mystery of the source, that which has absolutely no source.

The Son, while uncreated and fully God, is generated by the Father. To be created means to be brought into existence from a state of nonexistence. To be generated signifies that the Son receives his perfect existence eternally from the Father. The Son, as Word and Image, is the whole Trinity spoken by the Father. He is the mystery of the Father's utterance. In the Son, we contemplate the mystery of the Father's uttering or giving himself entirely, whose utterance perfectly images himself. The Holy Spirit, as Love and Gift, is the mystery of the Father and Son's unitive embrace. This divine Love proceeds as unfathomable embrace between the source and the image, the freely bestowed embrace of Love that, because of its perfectly free bestowal, is Gift. In the Holy Spirit, we contemplate the fruit of unfathomable self-giving.

The order of the Persons is therefore like a dance that reveals the personal characteristics within the unity of the movement. If we might turn from St. Thomas's theology to the poetic vision his theology inspired, consider how Dante beautifully evokes the Trinity and our deification in the incarnate Son:

Not that within the Living Light there was
    more than a sole aspect of the Divine
    which always is what It has always been,
yet as I learned to see more, and the power
    of vision grew in me, that single aspect
    as I changed, seemed to me to change Itself.
Within Its depthless clarity of substance
    I saw the Great Light shine into three circles
    in three clear colors bound in one same space;
the first seemed to reflect the next like rainbow
    on rainbow, and the third was like a flame
    equally breathed forth by the other two.
How my weak words fall short of my conception,
    which is itself so far from what I saw
    that "weak" is much too weak a word to use!
O Light Eternal fixed in Self alone,
    known only to Yourself, and knowing Self,
    You love and glow, knowing and being known!
That circling which, as I conceived it, shone
    in You as Your own first reflected light
    when I had looked deep into It a while,

seemed in Itself and in Its own Self-color
    to be depicted with man's very image.
    My eyes were totally absorbed in It.
As the geometer who tries so hard
    to square the circle, but cannot discover,
    think as he may, the principle involved,
so did I strive with this new mystery:
    I yearned to know how could our image fit
    into that circle, how it could conform;
but my own wings could not take me so high—
    then a great flash of understanding struck
    my mind, and suddenly its wish was granted.
At this point power failed high fantasy
    but, like a wheel in perfect balance turning,
    I felt my will and my desire impelled
by the Love that moves the sun and the other stars.[6]

The Trinity is this "wheel in perfect balance turning" in which Christ
enables us to participate eternally. We have reached the pinnacle of our
contemplative ascent. Squinting with Dante in the divine light, we experience a true glimpse of the inexhaustible mystery. The task of theology,
however, has only just begun. The Trinity has created and redeemed in
history through the temporal missions of the Son and the Holy Spirit. As
St. John tells the story,

> In the beginning was the Word, and the Word was with God, and
> the Word was God. He was in the beginning with God; all things
> were made through him, and without him was not anything made
> that was made. . . . And the Word became flesh and dwelt among
> us, full of grace and truth; we have beheld his glory, glory as of the
> only Son from the Father. . . . And from his fullness have we all
> received, grace upon grace. For the law was given through Moses;
> grace and truth came through Jesus Christ. No one has ever seen
> God; the only Son, who is in the bosom of the Father, he has made
> him known. (Jn 1:1–3, 14, 16–18)

---

6. Dante, *The Divine Comedy,* vol. 3: *Paradise,* trans. Mark Musa (New York:
Penguin, 1986), Canto 33 (pp. 392–394).

Or as St. Thomas says: "There are two reasons why the knowledge of the divine persons was necessary for us. It was necessary for the right idea of creation . . . [that God freely creates]. In another way, and chiefly, that we may think rightly concerning the salvation of the human race, accomplished by the Incarnate Son, and by the gift of the Holy Spirit" (1, q.32, a.1, ad 3). Since theology is the study of God and all things in relation to him, let us turn, for the remainder of this book, to the Trinity's gifts of creation and redemption.

CHAPTER TWO

CREATION, PROVIDENCE, AND SIN

Every now and again, one hears news reports about "creationists." Creationists refuse to admit that scientific advances have occurred in our understanding of the processes by which the universe's formation proceeded. Obviously such a viewpoint is deeply mistaken. Yet all Christians are creationists, in a sense! Fortunately, the negative connotations of "creationist" have nothing to do with St. Thomas's extraordinary teaching about creation. Let us heed the words of the Old Testament preacher Ecclesiastes, both somber and joyful: "Remember also your Creator in the days of your youth, before the evil days come . . . and the dust returns to the earth as it was, and the spirit returns to God who gave it" (Eccles 12:1, 7).

Creation and Analogy

With the words "In the beginning God created the heavens and the earth" (Gen 1:1), the biblical drama begins. Creation describes that decisive action by which God gave existence to creatures that had no prior existence. Yet creation does not merely point to some distant past event, but it tells us as well of God's continuing activity of bestowing being on his creation. The created universe utterly depends upon God; God, however, does not utterly depend upon the universe. As the

Psalmist declares, "Before the mountains were brought forth, or ever thou hadst formed the earth and the world, from everlasting to everlasting thou art God" (Ps 90:2). We should begin by reviewing this fundamental distinction between God and creatures, which we touched upon in the previous chapter.

What aspects characterize creaturely existence? The creatures that ordinarily confront us in experience of the world are material beings. They are composed of elements, and undergo material change. Their existence is limited to locations in space and time. They exist as multiples within a class: many bacteria, many rocks, many stars, many galaxies. They become perfect, or fail to do so, in terms of some kind of fulfillment proper to them. The distinction between God and creatures, nonetheless, is even greater. Spiritual creatures, such as angels, also exist. Their existence differs from the existence of material creatures. They are not composed of elements, and do not undergo change in any ordinary sense of the term. They are not limited to locations in space and time. They do not exist as multiples within a class. Yet however much their existence differs from the existence of material creatures, they are equally creatures.

The distinction between creatures and God thus is much more fundamental than any distinction that can be found among creatures. It is rather the difference between beings that have an origin of their existence and a being that does not. Creatures receive their existence from God who gives it to them, and so are not identical with their existence. They can begin to be, and may cease to be. God is his existence, and he can neither begin to be nor cease to be.

Consider further an example that we have already discussed: God is perfect. Does this mean that God is perfect in the way that creatures are? No. As we have seen, we have to be careful when we apply language to God, since none of our words, or concepts, can grasp the infinite nature of God. From our knowledge of creatures, we can only speak of something being perfect according to its kind—a perfect cow, or a perfect curve ball. God, however, is perfect being, perfect existence. Such perfection escapes the limits of our reason and even of our imagination. So, we use words such as "perfect" and "pure Act" to show that God's infinite existence is unimaginably greater than any existence we encounter through creatures.

Nonetheless, while affirming that God's perfections are ever-greater than the worldly perfections, St. Thomas holds that they are in a certain sense the *same* perfections. In the previous chapter, we pointed out that this does not mean that there is diversity in God that would destroy his simplicity. Since God is pure Act, "He must contain within himself the whole perfection of being" (1, q.4, a.3). Since creatures participate diversely in Act, they possess diverse perfections. These perfections, in the simplicity of pure Act, "pre-exist in God unitedly and simply" (1, q.13, a.4). God's essence, the divine Act, is therefore the "likeness" of all finite things. This is so because finite things exist by participation in Act.

One might ask how the real distinction between God and creatures is maintained if the perfections discernible in creatures preexist in God. How are the perfections possessed in a finite, diverse way by creatures possessed supereminently by God, without creatures thereby being God? St. Thomas uses the sun to illustrate this relationship. He notes that "things generated by the sun's heat may be in some sort spoken of as like the sun," because they have heat. The relation of creatures to God is even more distant: while hot things are "likenesses" of the sun that generates them, since both sun and thing are hot, created things are likenesses of the Creator not by sharing what the Creator is (infinite being) but by a certain *likeness* to infinite being (1, q.4, a.3). St. Thomas reminds us that this likeness is "by way of a certain assimilation which is far removed and defective" (1, q.7, a.4). The likeness of creatures to God is not a correspondence, but rather an analogous likeness based on the relation of effect to cause. Finite cannot be proportional to infinite. On this basis, St. Thomas remarks, "Although it may be admitted that creatures are in some sort like God, it must nowise be admitted that God is like creatures" (1, q.4, a.3, ad 4). He thus illumines how the being of creatures depends absolutely upon God and is entirely present in God, without God's being thereby depending upon creatures.

God and Creation

After analyzing the distinction between the Creator and the creation, we now turn to examine further how the creation depends upon God.

The opening chapters of Genesis are not the only passages from Scripture describing creation. The New Testament has its creation story as well: "In the beginning was the Word, and the Word was with God, and the Word was God. He was in the beginning with God; all things were made through him, and without him was not anything that was made" (Jn 1:1–3). Here we have the revelation that God was not a solitary in the act of creation. It is true that the divine Persons are not distinguished in anything but their mutual relations, and so the divine Persons act as one in creating. Yet the order of the Persons shapes the character of the action. St. Thomas states that "God the Father made the creature through his Word, which is his Son; and through his Love, which is the Holy Spirit" (1, q.45, a.6). It is not for nothing that his discussion of creation follows immediately after his treatment of the Holy Trinity. Although the processions in God are God, whereas creatures are not God, nonetheless knowledge of the Trinity illumines our knowledge of creation. In the processions of the divine Persons, we find the "type," or model, of the procession of creatures from God. The eternal processions of wisdom and love teach us that God the Trinity freely knows and loves us into existence. God, as a communion of Persons, does not need the world, but rather by the superabundance of his goodness freely wills that the world come into being. He does not love us because he needs us, but rather loves us into being without constraint or restriction.

God who is infinite being creates a world of finite beings. Thus, all beings apart from God are not their own being, but instead receive their being from God. This is known as the doctrine of *participation*. In a finite way, creatures participate, or share in, the pure being of God. Whatever exists, then, is caused by God. Yet creatures can be more or less perfect insofar as they participate more or less in the sheer existence of God. When we speak of creation in the modern world, we typically think of what St. Thomas would have called efficient causality. Something is an efficient cause if it is the force that leads something else to occur. For example, the combustion of gasoline is the efficient cause of Jane's car driving around town.

God the Trinity creates the world as efficient cause. He does so in a radical sense. To work on something requires that there be some preexisting material. Since God, however, creates everything from nothing (*creatio ex nihilo*), there is no preexisting material upon which God works (1, q.45, a.2). The universe simply does not exist before God creates. To speak precisely, then, creation actually involves no work. God does not have to change something from one state to another. It is not as if there are things in a state of "nothing" that God has to change into a state of being. The Book of Genesis captures this reality by describing creation in terms of God speaking, and things coming to be (Gen 1). God creates through his Word.

The concept of efficient causality, therefore, is not adequate by itself to describe the way the world is created by God. A deeper understanding of causality is needed. To extend the example of driving, we might ask why Jane is driving around at all, or what is the purpose of Jane's driving. Perhaps in this case Jane is driving her car to buy a book at the bookstore. This is the "final cause," or intended goal, of Jane's driving. Every intelligent action has a final cause, or goal.

Another kind of causality is called "exemplar cause." This refers to the pattern or form that makes something be a particular kind of thing. What is the pattern according to which God creates? Or, to use the language loosely, what are the blueprints for the universe (exemplar cause)? Why did God create anything at all (final cause)?

How is God the "exemplar cause" of creation? Following an insight of St. Augustine, St. Thomas saw in the Platonic doctrine of forms a disclosure of the truth that the form or pattern of every created being exists in the mind of God. The ultimate standard, then, for judging anything in the world exists outside the world in God. This idea leads in two directions. First, in arriving at understanding of any creature, we are led back to a perfection in God. Second, and conversely, we must recognize that the true essence of any creature is beyond our complete comprehension since its true essence is only known by God. In our knowledge of the world, there is both knowing and unknowing. Because things in this world are created by God, God alone knows their complete pattern or nature. St. Thomas therefore offers a middle path between modernity's passion for objectivity and postmodernity's view that truth is a mere human construction, without any real ground. God alone has complete knowledge of any created thing, yet we as creatures to whom he has given rational faculties can come to know—even if only partially—the truth about what he has created. God, who is supremely knowable (even if our weak intellects are not capable of grasping his infinite light), creates things which are intelligible—that is, intrinsically capable of being understood. The mind does not impose its "categories of understanding" upon things. Rather, in manifesting their being, things reveal themselves as knowable.

God is not only the exemplar cause of everything, he is also the final cause of everything. Final causality answers the question "why." God created the world to communicate his goodness. As St. Bonaventure, a contemporary of St. Thomas, said, "God created the world to share his glory." Creatures exist in order to reach the perfection that is appropriate to their kind. A flower's perfection is different than a lion's, which is different than a supernova's. When created things reach their full potential, they can be said to exist in the fullest manner. Thus, each created thing aims at reaching the goodness proper to its being. If we recall the doctrine of participation, we can see that the goodness proper to each thing participates in God's perfect goodness. As each created thing arrives at its own goodness, it participates more in God's perfect goodness. God's goodness, thus, is the end toward which all things are directed. This does not mean, of course, that God created in order to increase his goodness, as if that were possible. On the contrary, God alone "is the most perfectly liberal giver, because he does not act for his own profit, but only for his own goodness" (1, q.44, a.4, ad 1).

The doctrine of creation thus does not merely tell us where the world came from. It tells us as well where the world is going. Creation comes forth from God in order to return to God. The world did not emanate from God by necessity, as the Neoplatonist philosophers thought; it was created by the free and loving will of God. In God's will and wisdom, he created the world so that it might find its perfection in returning to him. This is the biblical understanding of creation depicted in such passages as Psalm 19:1, "The heavens are telling the glory of God," and Psalm 150:6, "Let everything that breathes praise the Lord!"

St. Thomas structures his entire *Summa Theologiae* along this pattern of creation going forth from God and returning to him. Theology thus treats God not simply as he exists in himself, but as the beginning and end of all creatures, especially of rational creatures, including both angels and human beings. The *Summa Theologiae* has three main parts. The first part is dedicated to God as one and three and to creation as coming forth from him. The second part treats "the rational creature's advance towards God" (1, q.2, prologue). We advance back toward God by means of actions informed by the virtues, above all by the virtue of charity. The third part presents "Christ, Who as man, is our way to God" (ibid.). Through Christ and the sacraments he instituted, human beings can reach their ultimate purpose in knowing and loving God.

Providence and Predestination

Many views of creation have been infected with a deistic view of a creator that limits God's role to the beginning of the universe. Much as someone might wind up an old-fashioned clock and let it wind down, God, according to the deistic view, sets the universe in motion and then stands back. This deistic view, however, is alien to the biblical view of God as expressed in the theology of St. Thomas. Creation, instead, names an ongoing relationship by which creatures receive their existence at each moment from the Creator.

We have already examined how in God is the perfection of every creature. Both the standard, or exemplar, by which the thing was created and the goal toward which the thing is striving exist in God. Not only does God know the origin and purpose of each created thing, he also directs the process by which each thing moves from its origin to achieving its purpose. We call this direction divine providence.

Providence is God's prudence or practical wisdom. Prudence is the knowledge of the right end as well as the knowledge of the right means to attain that end. Prudence also requires that this knowledge lead to proper action. More than merely knowing what to do, and even knowing how to do it, prudence actually does it. As a form of prudence, divine providence thus includes both the order of all things (knowing what and knowing how) and the execution of that order (actually doing it). The first exists eternally in God; the second is God's temporal action in governing the universe. God's execution of his providence includes both chance and necessity. Some things happen by necessity—an apple falls to the ground. Others happen by contingency—a man decides he wants to marry this woman instead of that woman. From the perspective of the twenty-first century, contingent causes would also include everything from chaos theory to the uncertainty principle associated with quantum mechanics.

Does God's providence extend to every created thing? Jesus teaches in the affirmative, "Even the hairs on your head are numbered" (Mt 10:30). The details of human history may sometimes make it seem that life were merely "a tale told by an idiot, full of sound and fury, signifying nothing" (*Macbeth* V, 5). It is very significant, however, that Macbeth speaks these words at the moment the horrible consequences of his sin are being revealed. Macbeth's own situation, with the justice that is being accomplished, is Shakespeare's eloquent testimony to the reality of God's providential order. As we will see, God's providence allows for the misuse of human freedom, but God's purpose (the "final cause" of creation) is not thereby thwarted—although this will become clear fully only at the end of time, when all has been accomplished. For now, as Ecclesiastes says, "he has made everything beautiful in its time; also he has put eternity into man's mind, yet so that he cannot find out what God has done from the beginning to the end" (Eccles 3:11). But in the Book of Revelation, the saints at the final judgment sing, "Great and wonderful are thy deeds, O Lord God the Almighty! Just and true are thy ways, O King of the ages! Who shall not fear and glorify thy name, O Lord? For thou alone art holy. All nations shall come and worship thee, for thy judgments have been revealed" (Rev 15:3–4).

To grasp the working of divine providence, one needs to distinguish between divine and natural causality, or between primary and secondary causality. God as Creator is the primary cause, but because of his goodness, he gives his creatures the power to act as true causes in the world, albeit secondary causes. St. Thomas writes that "the dignity of causality is imparted even to creatures" (1, q.22, a.3). We should attribute any effect or action in the world both to God as the principal cause—in the ways we have discussed above—and to nature as the instrumental, secondary cause. This does not mean that the effect comes 50 percent from God and 50 percent from nature. Instead, the effect is 100 percent from God as the principal agent and 100 percent from nature as the instrumental agent. Thus, to the question of why did the apple fall onto Newton's head, we may answer because of the law of gravity and we may also answer because God, in willing creation, willed that the apple should fall.

The significance of the distinction between primary and secondary causes becomes especially apparent in the contemporary debates concerning the evolution of species. If evolution—the common ancestry of all forms of life—has occurred, and if it has occurred according to an interaction of the laws of nature and chance, then this would simply explain instrumental causality. Those who wish to investigate primary causality would have to ask *from where* the laws of nature come. As we have seen, when St. Thomas asks whether God exists, he responds that since nature always works toward particular ends, "whatever is done by nature must be traced back to God, as to its first cause" (1, q.2, a.3, ad 2). No law of nature or exercise of human free will can explain the existence of nature or of human free will. All of modern science's advances in knowledge and explanation thus would have caused no crisis of faith for St. Thomas. The more intricate becomes our knowledge of the world, the more powerful the demand that we recognize that God must be at work in and through the world.

More needs to be said, however, about the interaction of divine providence and human free will. We have already asserted that God's providence can work through necessary and contingent causes. Nevertheless, to many observers it appears contradictory to assert that God's will acts through human free will. How can we have free will if God is acting through us? Would not this make us puppets? St. Thomas answers that God alone can move our will without violating its integrity. If any human being were to move our will—as in the case of brainwashing—then this would be incompatible with our own choosing. God, however, created our will and instilled it with a natural "order" toward choosing what we see to be good. Since God has granted the origin and purpose of our will, he also moves our will—*by enabling it to move*—to choose freely what appears good to us. Since God is the Creator and we are his creatures, we are in a noncompetitive relationship with God. His actions do not take away from our actions. His act makes it possible for us to act at all!

The above has described what is known as God's general providence of creation. There remains to be discussed God's selective providence of human beings to eternal life with God. This is called God's predestination. It is important not to imagine "predestination" as if God were like a movie director who plans the action and then sits back and watches the actors do what he has arranged for them to do (cf. St. Thomas's *De Veritate* 2, 12). On the contrary, God is in eternity, not in time; there is absolutely no "before" or "after" in God, who is eternal Presence.

Predestination, then, must be completely distinguished from the idolatrous concept of a god who watches his creatures do what "beforehand" he knew they would do. Instead, divine providence is God's practical wisdom of the origin and purpose of creatures, as well as the "ordering" of them to achieve that purpose. Divine predestination is distinguished from divine providence because God has created angels and human beings with a purpose that exceeds their respective natural capacities. Our purpose is eternal life, which consists in seeing God. Since the goal of human life exceeds human capabilities, we require God's direct assistance in order to reach our goal. God's general providence works in and through all created natures; God's predestination of human beings to glory works in and through us and gives us capacities exceeding our nature. We call this new life, which gives us a sharing in God's trinitarian life far beyond anything our natural capacities could have attained, the life of grace.

St. Thomas distinguishes between predestination and reprobation. The term "predestination" describes God actively causing, by the interior movement of grace in human persons, some human beings to enjoy eternal life. "Predestination" indicates that the only way we can arrive at this glorious destiny is for God to enable us to attain it. The term "reprobation" refers to God permitting some human beings to suffer eternal punishment.

Predestination "is the cause both of what is expected in the future life by the predestined—namely, glory—and of what is received in this life—namely, grace. Reprobation, however, is not the cause of what is in the present—namely, sin; but it is the cause . . . of what is assigned in the future—namely, eternal punishment" (1, q.23, a.3, ad 2). Human sin, which is not caused by God, is what leads to eternal punishment. God thus directly acts to predestine to glory, but God does not directly act to damn to Hell. God's predestination permits that some may choose to reject his offer of grace.

God respects the dignity of human free will to such an extent that he allows human beings to choose themselves and their own false world instead of choosing God and the real world. Those who go to Hell do so because they choose it. As St. Thomas says, "guilt proceeds from the free will of the person who is reprobated and deserted by grace. In this way the word of the prophet is true—namely, *Destruction is thy own, O Israel* [Hos 13:9]" (1, q.23, a.3, ad 2). In short, God is the cause of eternal life in those who choose it, and God permits others to choose themselves. Although divine predestination covers both aspects, we can say that predestination more properly refers to God's active predestination to glory. This is how St. Paul speaks of predestination, "those whom [God] predestined, he also called" (Rom 8:30).

Man as Created in the Image of God

Among created beings, humankind stands at the center of theological inquiry, because God took on a human nature in Jesus Christ. Nonetheless, God created rational creatures other than human beings. These are angels—spiritual beings possessing intellect and will, yet lacking any material existence. The paintings of men with wings are perhaps the best way of depicting creatures that have no material image. Nonetheless, this image is woefully inadequate. As pure spirits, angels have a power of intellect and a force of will greatly surpassing anything in the best and brightest of the human species.

God also created material beings possessing neither intellect nor will—irrational creatures, such as rocks, plants, and animals. To call animals, such as your dog, irrational is not an insult. St. Thomas was aware that animals are sentient and have feelings, memories, dreams, and communication. As Alasdair MacIntyre has recently argued, animals may hold beliefs about their surrounding environment. What classifies them as irrational is their inability to reflect on those beliefs.

At the nexus of the spiritual creation (angels) and the material creation (rocks, plants, dogs) stands the human creature possessing both spirit and matter. We share with rocks the fact that we exist in space and time, with plants that we live and grow, and with dogs that we live, move about in the world, and are sentient. We share with angels our rational soul, including both reason and will.

The first chapters of Genesis depict the unique character of man in creation. Unlike other material beings, human beings are stamped with the image of God. Genesis 1:27 famously reads, "God created man in his own image, in the image of God he created him; male and female he created them." Our creation in the image of God indubitably forms one of the central Christian convictions about who man is and where he is going. Man is made *in* the image of God, but Jesus Christ alone simply is "the image of the invisible God" (Col 1:15). The Son of God is the perfect image of the Father. We are imperfect, or incomplete, images of God—children of God by grace. As created in the image of God, man is like God. In what does this likeness consist? St. Thomas teaches that this likeness lies in our intellectual nature or rational soul. Our soul is the "form" of our body, which is another way of saying that the soul is the animating and organizing principle of the body. Soul and body are profoundly related in the unity of the human being. However, it is particularly our capacity to know and to love that makes us like God. But the question remains—who or what are we to know and to love? Since God is infinitely happy in knowing and loving himself, human beings imitate God when we are actively knowing and loving God.

The image of God is in the human creature in three ways: by nature, by grace, and in glory. First, simply with respect to what belongs to human nature, there is a natural capacity for knowing and understanding God. Any rational creature possesses this capacity. Each human being thus is said to be in the image of God.

Second, the image of God becomes more perfect when the human being is not simply capable of knowing and loving God, but is actually doing so. Grace makes it possible for man to reenter this relationship with God. Consider the case of a mirror: a mirror always has the capacity to reflect a face, but it requires the presence of light in order to fulfill its potential. Grace is the light of the soul enabling us to know and to love God. As we noted above, revelation offers new sensible realities, such as the revelation of the Trinity at Jesus' baptism, along with a greater intellectual light with which to perceive these realities, namely, the light of grace (1, q.12, a.13). The normal structure of human knowing remains the same: by an intellectual light, we perceive sensible realities. Revelation offers the light of grace to perceive the sensible realities of God's marvelous deeds. Yet, even this relationship is imperfect since our knowledge and love are imperfect.

Third, we have the case of those who see God in the glory of heaven. Since they know and love God perfectly, they possess the fullness of the image of God. We can speak of these three levels as the image of *creation,* which is common to all human beings, the image of *re-creation,* which is in those justified by grace, and the image of total *likeness,* which is only in the blessed in heaven.

Now the God in whose image we are created is a unity and a trinity. Human beings thus image both the divine essence and the divine trinity. St. Thomas here shows his mastery of both the Western and Eastern Fathers of the Church. St. John Damascene, from the East, writes that the image of God is in man as "an intelligent being endowed with free-will and self-movement" (1-2, prologue). Free will and self-movement belong to the divine essence or to the oneness of God. St. Augustine and St. Hilary of Poitiers, from the West, teach that the image of God in man is the image of the Trinity. As Augustine argues in *On the Trinity,* in man we see a trinity of the mind and the dual processions of knowledge and love (as well as the trinity of memory, understanding, and will). The view of John Damascene—the image of the unity of God—and the view of Augustine—the image of the Trinity of Persons—complement one another. If God is three and one and we are created in his image, then we are created in the image of the unity of essence and in the image of the plurality of persons.

Created in the image of God, human beings are created *in* and *for* a relationship with God. Only in this relationship can man find happiness. "You have put off the old nature with its practices and have put on the new nature, which is being renewed in knowledge after the image of its creator" (Col 3: 9–10).

Sin

If humankind was created in God's image and destined for glory, what happened? Why do violence, greed, pride, lust, and so forth seem so often to overwhelm our rational faculties? The Bible depicts the problem in symbolic terms: "So when the woman saw that the tree was good for food, and that it was a delight to the eyes, and that the tree was to be desired to make one wise, she took of its fruit and ate; and she also gave some to her husband, and he ate" (Gen 3:6–7). In the biblical account, which describes human freedom and the consequent ability to choose self over God (the sin of pride), God is described as having given the first human beings access to all the trees in the garden of Eden but one. Oblivious to God's extraordinary love, and with the suggestion of the devil, Adam and Eve imagined that this law was bad for them, and they sought to "be like God" (Gen 3:5) by usurping God's role as orderer of creation.

The history of creation suffered an earthquake at this event. Human beings were created in the image of God. St. Thomas explains that God granted the first human beings not merely a natural image, but also a graced image by which they were actually loving and knowing God. Nature refers to certain capacities and activities that are proper to human nature—whatever belongs to a creature with a rational soul and a body. Grace refers to capacities and activities that are above human nature— namely, a sharing in the very life of God. Both nature and grace are gifts from God, since all creation is a gift. Nevertheless, grace constitutes an unparalleled gift since it leads the creature to become like God—the process of divinization or deification, the purpose of creation.

We were created with nature and grace, but original sin damages our nature and destroys our grace. The supernatural life, or grace, leaves the human creature as the result of original sin. In the state of original justice, human beings had been upheld by grace from suffering bodily corruption. After original sin, there is no longer any impediment to the decay of our bodies through aging and disease. The natural life does not leave completely, but rather suffers a terrible wound. The human intellect no longer can see the truth about the world and God clearly. The human will can no longer choose decisively the true good. The intellect becomes darkened and the heart grows cold. Much as common experience might suggest, St. Thomas observes that "human nature is more corrupt by sin in regard to the desire for good, than in regard to the knowledge of truth" (1-2, q.109, a.2, ad 3). Original sin leaves humanity with a wounded nature and—what is even more devastating—the loss of grace that alone enables us to achieve the purpose for which we were created, that is, life with God.

But how is it that the sin of Adam and Eve affects us so deeply? Why are we guilty of a sin that was committed long before we existed?

St. Thomas is a great help in understanding this mystery. Some earlier theologians had suggested that original sin was transmitted through pro-creation. Yet the physical elements of procreation cannot be the whole cause of the transmission of a condition of the *spiritual* soul. More impor-tant, even if we inherit a defect from our individual origin, how can we be guilty since the fact we were conceived was clearly involuntary on our part? The answer is found when we recognize that, in a sense, the whole human race is like one man. St. Paul frequently contrasts Adam and Christ. He writes, "as sin came into the world through one man and death through sin, . . . so death spread to all men because all men sinned. . . . If many died through one man's trespass, much more have the grace of God and the free gift in the grace of that one man Jesus Christ abounded for many" (Rom 5:12, 15). Since we have all inherited the same nature from Adam, together we form one man in Adam. Human beings are to Adam as individual members are to the body. Just as a murder committed by a hand is only voluntary because of the rational soul, so our original sin is only voluntary because of Adam.

Original sin therefore is not the sin of the individual person except insofar as we receive our nature from our first parent. The doctrine of original sin does not signify that we are guilty of a particular action, but that we suffer from the loss of that for which we were originally created. St. Thomas succinctly describes original sin as "the privation of original justice" (1, q.82, a.4).

Moving from original sin to actual sin, it is helpful to distinguish between mortal and venial sins. Mortal sins break the person's union with God, and thus destroy the life of grace. As in the story of the prodigal son, the sinner demands his inheritance, thus rupturing any relationship to his father (Lk 15). Venial sins are still offensive against God and right rea-son: "All wrongdoing is sin, but there is sin which is not mortal" (1 Jn 5:17). Although the soul is disordered by venial sins, it has not turned away from God. Venial sins weaken charity without destroying it.

Mortal sin is characterized by an action or a deliberate thought in a grave matter or in a lesser matter done in grave way. The mere thought of a sinful pleasure lacks the firmness of a mortal sin. Yet the consent to dwell on a sinful thought is a sin. As one spiritual author put it, you cannot pre-vent a bird from landing in your hair, but you can keep it from building a nest there. This is how St. Thomas interprets Jesus' teaching, "I say to you that everyone who looks at a woman lustfully has already committed adultery with her in his heart" (Mt 5:28). The free *consent* to fantasize about adultery would be a mortal sin since adultery is a mortal sin. It is important to see that the distinction between mortal and venial sin is not merely a juridical one. Rather, the distinction serves to give us confidence that our many falls do not necessarily break our relationship to God. Yet, all sins require repentance and forgiveness of sins through Jesus Christ.

Sin must be understood within the context of creation and providence. We must completely rid ourselves of the view of God as a failed "inventor" of humanity. People sometimes ask why God created human beings if, in his eternal Presence, he knew they would sin. Some view this as foolish on God's part; others see it as calling into doubt God's goodness since he creates us knowing that we will incur punishment for violating our relationship with him. Yet, since God is pure Act and therefore utterly transcends space and time, he embraces each moment and each part of his creation in his perfect and eternal existence. In creating man, God not only knows that man will sin, he also knows that he will offer salvation to man through the Incarnation of the Word. Speaking of God's eternity embracing each moment is simply another way of expressing the biblical understanding of "the book of life of the Lamb that was slain" that was "written before the foundation of the world" (Rev 13:8). Although we cannot speak of a "before" in God, we can affirm that the cure of the Incarnation is greater than the disease of sin. Following the tradition, St. Thomas describes the Fall as a *felix culpa,* quoting the Exultet, a song from the Easter liturgy: "O happy fault, O necessary sin of Adam, that has merited for us so great a Redeemer!"

CHAPTER THREE

HAPPINESS AND VIRTUE

Ecclesiastes is famous for saying, "I have seen everything that is done under the sun; and behold, all is vanity and a striving after wind" (Eccles 1:14). It might seem that Ecclesiastes was a bit pessimistic. After all, a football game with tailgate parties might be, in the broad picture of things, "vanity and a striving after wind," but nonetheless fun and relaxing. Should Ecclesiastes have lightened up? Not at all. In fact, his words speak to the depths of our hearts. Beyond the fleeting delights and disturbances of the day, we are searching for friendship that cannot be shaken, in which we can truly love and be loved. Have you ever had the feeling after somehow hurting a friend— say, by gossiping about her—that you wish you could become a better friend? Have you ever wished that you could learn how to become, not just a friend, but a true friend, one whose love would be permanent and whose love would be permanently reciprocated?

What constitutes a "good person"? How can we become friends, lovers, who truly love our neighbors even when love requires difficult words and actions? Can we be made worthy of an eternal friendship, friendship with God? In Christian theology, these questions—asked also by ancient philosophers and people of all times and places—take on a special depth and poignancy, since Jesus teaches his disciples that they will be truly happy, or blessed, if they do what he commands

(Jn 13:17). St. Thomas begins his discussion of the good life—what it means truly to become a "good person"—by asking not about rules, but about what constitutes true happiness and the virtuous life.

Happiness in God

All people desire happiness, but many fail to attain it. In Henry David Thoreau's famous phrase, "The mass of men live lives of quiet desperation." We readily admit that the possession of money, cars, and houses will not satisfy. Experiences of sporting events, concerts, meeting celebrities, and sexual intercourse—to name the experiences that savvy advertisers focus on to sell their products—evaporate quickly into yesterday and provide not only no lasting satisfaction, but frequently dissatisfaction. The more reflective among us might argue that happiness lies in human friendships, monogamous marriage, and serving others in general. Yet even relationships with other people do not truly give the lasting happiness we desire, since as sinners we are continually betraying even our closest friends—as any honest married couple will tell you—and moreover death means that these friendships will not last in this world. To be *truly* happy, indeed, a person would need to have no fear of losing the present happiness.

We might conclude, therefore, that happiness is simply unattainable. Yet the Psalmist announces otherwise: "Blessed is the man who walks not in the counsel of the wicked, nor stands in the sinners, nor sits in the set of scoffers; but his delight is in the law of the Lord, and on his law he meditates day and night" (Ps 1:1–2). In the psalm, the man who seeks the Lord and follows his law is rightly called blessed. Happiness here does not mean the immediate gratification of desire; it means the fulfillment of the deepest longings of the human soul to know the truth and to possess the good, to love and to be loved. The Psalmist tells us that God *can* satisfy us; the Psalmist also suggests that God *alone* can satisfy us. Since God is eternal, he can provide the lasting happiness that all created things cannot deliver. Since he is infinite goodness and infinite truth, he can satisfy every desire we have to know what is true and to love what is good. As St. Augustine states in his *Confessions*, "You have made us for yourself, O Lord, and our hearts are restless until they rest in you" (book 1, chap. 1).

St. Thomas, then, holds that nothing else than intellectual or spiritual union with God will make us happy. As 1 John teaches, "it does not yet appear what we shall be, but we know that when he appears we shall be like him, for we shall see him as he is" (1 Jn 3:2). We have been created for infinite love, truth, and joy. Our rational natures will remain incomplete apart from knowing the truth and loving the good. God, however, created us for even more than that. He created us in the grace of divine sonship, which we lost through sin. Since this is what we are created for, if we fail to live as sons and daughters of God, then our lives properly can be considered failures; we have not reached our purpose. We were not created to live only a natural life as a rational creature; we were created to live a supernatural life with God. Because of sin, there is nothing we can do on our own to be worthy to call God "Father." Behind all that we will say about happiness and virtue in this chapter, therefore, lies the fact that Christ has come into the world to save us from our sins and give us the grace of adoption as children of God: "And because you are sons, God has sent the Spirit of his Son into our hearts, crying 'Abba! Father!'" (Gal 4:6).

All human beings desire happiness; so far so good. All desire happiness from whatever they think will make them happy; so far *not* so good! St. Thomas recognizes that we have the freedom to choose what appears good to us. If this apparent good, however, is not truly good for us, then it is incapable of making us happy. As Proverbs 14:12 says, "There is a way which seems right to a man, but its end is the way of death." The necessary thing is to learn how to live in a way that leads to the happiness we are made for: infinite love, truth, and joy. We cannot simply decide that we *want* infinite love, truth, and joy. We must, by choosing goods that are truly perfective of our being, *become* people who are able to recognize and embrace love, truth, and joy. For example, until we learn the habits and skills needed for reading books, we will not be able to enjoy *War and Peace*. The same thing holds for true happiness. To be happy in the fullest sense, we must acquire habits conducive to living in a way that enables us to be all that God has made us to be. Absent certain habits and skills, reality will seem to us to be singularly uninspiring and confusing, even frustrating. Following a long tradition, St. Thomas calls the habits and skills necessary to be happy—to live joyfully in truth and love, even when suffering—"virtues."

Human Action

Before discussing virtues, however, we need to discuss the structure of human *acts,* since to possess a virtue means to act well. What is it that makes a human action distinct from the actions of other creatures? Also, what distinguishes moral actions—actions that are good or bad—from other actions that human beings do, such as digesting a filet mignon or scratching one's ear while reading a book? St. Thomas holds that moral actions, or human actions properly speaking, are voluntary, that is, they are done for the sake of an end, for some purpose. Properly *human* actions, involving intellect and free will, are those actions which if you asked the person performing the action (the "agent" of the act), "Why are you doing that?" the person could give an answer. For example, when asked why she went to the bookstore, Jane could answer, "To buy a book on the theology of St. Thomas Aquinas." Her action has an intentional purpose.

There are three parts to any given action: *the intention, the object, and the circumstances.* To evaluate actions, we must examine all three parts. The intention of the act is why we are doing it. The object of the act is the accurate description of what we are immediately doing. The circumstances of the act form all of the details surrounding the act that are neither the intention nor the object, but nonetheless alter the character of the act. St. Thomas notes that for an action to be considered right, it must be good with respect to all three aspects—its intention, its object, and its circumstances. An action is wrong if it fails in any of the three parts. Consider the case of paying a friend $500 for a ten-year-old pickup truck. First, what is the intention? To acquire cheap transportation to and from a job or to use the truck in a terrorist attack? Second, what is the object of the act? Do you give your friend legitimate or counterfeit currency? Third, what are the circumstances of the act? If you are ten years old, should you really be driving a truck? Buying the pickup truck becomes a bad action if it fails in any one of the above categories.

St. Thomas holds, therefore, that it is not morally permissible to do something evil (a bad object) for a good reason (a good intention). The action would be wrong *regardless* of the intention. There are intrinsically evil acts that can never be justified whatever the circumstances or consequences—adultery, murder, apostasy, and so on. The martyrs exemplify the refusal to commit the sin of denying Christ even while knowing that death will result. St. Paul shows this when he asks not do evil so that good may come?" (Rom 3:8). The ity of the act is judged in terms of the object of the act. intentions, nonetheless, are required to come to a full ction.

For an action to be judged a good action, it must be done for the right reason, the action itself must be good, and it must be done in the right circumstances. Consider the act of serving a meal at a homeless shelter. The object of the act is undeniably good—feeding the hungry. Yet it must be done for the right intention. Feeding the hungry is hardly praiseworthy if it is only done to pad one's résumé. Finally, the circumstances must be acceptable as well. If a husband were at a soup kitchen while he knew his wife was having a baby at the hospital, the act would be a wrong act. The husband would be doing the right thing, but at the wrong time. As T. S. Eliot wrote, "It is a tragic thing to do the right thing for the wrong reason."

> Intellect, will, heart
> Mr. Lizardo's theory

Passionate Beings

St. Thomas does not, however, see human beings as purely intellectual creatures. We do not act merely because of knowledge of what we desire; we act because of our passions as well. There are two main sources of human action: the intellect and will on the one hand, and the passions on the other. St. Thomas, in fact, devotes far more questions to the latter. In this discussion, passion refers not merely to sexual passion, but to a broad range of passions, or what could also be called the broad spectrum of emotions: love, hatred, delight, lust, sorrow, hope, despair, fear, daring, and anger. Passions arise from our bodily nature and are appetites or desires to do a certain thing.

St. Thomas divides the passions or emotions into two categories of the appetite: the "concupiscible" appetite and the "irascible" appetite. The concupiscible appetite covers all of the desires that we have in the presence of some good thing. When faced with chocolate, we feel moved to eat it. The irascible appetite covers the resistance to difficulties and evils. This is what is commonly known as the "flight or fight" response mechanism. All of the emotions and passions, both those for pursuing the good (concupiscible) and those for resisting difficulties (irascible), are given to us from God. They are part of the human creature that God declared to be "very good" (Gen 1:31).

Here we find a fourth facet of St. Thomas's understanding of moral actions. It is not enough to do the right action, with the right intentions, in the right circumstances. A perfect action will be done with the right emotions. This may sound strange to modern ears. We are used to saying that our feelings and emotions are not in our control. Immanuel Kant, the eighteenth-century German philosopher, went so far as to judge an action better if the agent did not enjoy what he or she was doing. Nonetheless, the classical and Christian approach has included in the moral life the cultivation of certain emotions. St. Paul commands Christians, "Rejoice in the Lord always; again I will say, Rejoice" (Phil 4:4). Not only does he demand certain emotions, he then warns against other ones: "Have no anxiety about anything" (Phil 4:6).

Recall that the whole question of the moral life, for St. Thomas, falls within our quest for happiness. What kind of actions will lead us to true happiness with God and what kind of actions will not? Once this context is remembered, it is easier to see the moral significance of the emotions. Who is happier? A missionary priest in a poor village in Latin America who longs to return home, or one who deeply enjoys his life there? If the goal is the fulfillment of our nature and, even more, a sharing in God's nature, then our emotional lives must be shaped in certain ways for us to reach our goal.

Sometimes we have to lead with our wills and hope that our emotions will follow. In her autobiography, St. Teresa of Avila relates that when she first began to care for the poor she was full of dislike and disgust for them. With time and prayer, however, she developed an intense affection for each of the people she cared for. Although our emotions are not completely under our control, we have a responsibility to cultivate certain emotions and struggle against others. The moral life is more than becoming a good person by following the rules. It consists in making progress toward perfect happiness. We know from the Christian faith that we cannot attain perfection or freedom from sin in this life, so we must struggle toward the goal and rely upon God's help. The struggle certainly is great, but the assistance is even greater. As St. Paul teaches, "work out your own salvation with fear and trembling; for God is at work in you, both to will and to work for his good pleasure" (Phil 2:12–13).

The Virtues

Good actions are steps along the way to true happiness. But some people are more likely to perform good actions than other people. This is what we mean by a person's character. If the character is good, the person will reliably act well. If the character is bad, the person will just as reliably act poorly. Good habits or good characteristics are called virtues; bad habits or bad characteristics are called vices. Moreover, St. Thomas emphasizes that virtuous persons are not islands of goodness, cut off from each other. Instead, *friendships* are intrinsic to possessing the virtues. To attain true happiness we must become a true friend, and we need friends who help us in this quest. The greatest such friend is Jesus Christ, our Lord and teacher. The virtues, in their fullest sense, describe the kind of person who is, by grace, a friend of God!

St. Thomas sees virtues as the perfecting of certain capacities within the person to do what is good. All people may be capable of doing good, but they will not actually be able to do so unless they are practiced in it or have received it as a gift from God. For instance, any person with adequate hearing and a sufficient number of fingers has the capacity to play the piano. Ears and fingers, however, do not suffice to make a pianist. A two-year-old may bang on the keys, but we call it "banging on the keys" for a reason. The capacity to play the piano is worthless unless that capacity is developed through practice. By some mixture of talent and training, some people come to possess the skill of playing the piano. Once possessed, this skill is distinct from the action of playing the piano since the person still has the skill even whether playing or not.

[margin note: capacity, skill, and action]

So too with the virtues. The virtues are the skills of acting well that the virtuous person possesses whether engaged in a specific good action or not. Just as pianists can be counted on to play the piano should the need arise, virtuous persons can be counted on to perform good actions in whatever situations they encounter. When St. Thomas speaks of a virtue as a good "habit," he does not mean that a virtue is something done without thought or merely "out of habit." The word "habit" here means the reliable disposition or acquired skill that enables one to act well on a consistent basis.

We can define virtue in various ways. The *Catechism of the Catholic Church* defines virtue as "the habitual and firm disposition to do the good." St. Thomas uses the definition provided by St. Augustine, who described virtue as "a good quality of the mind, by which we live righteously, of which no one can make bad use, which God works in us, without us" (*On Free Will* 2, 19). This definition highlights a crucial aspect of the virtues. The noblest virtues are not the ones we acquire on our own, but those God grants to us through the grace of the Incarnation. This is

[margin note: definitions of virtue]

what Augustine means by "which God works in us, without us." These godly virtues are necessary to attain the goal of human life, which extends beyond human nature.

Natural and Supernatural Virtues

Virtues are the perfection of powers of the human soul. Since God bestows both nature and grace, there are two principles of human life: the natural life and the supernatural life (the life of grace). The "moral" virtues perfect the natural life and the "theological" virtues perfect the supernatural life. What makes this picture more complex, however, is that the natural life and the supernatural life do not exist as two separate planes of existence. Instead, they interpenetrate each other. The supernatural life reaches down to heal and to elevate the natural life without destroying its integrity. For example, Christ has elevated marriage into a sacrament of his grace. Christian marriage, nevertheless, has many aspects belonging simply to the natural order of marriage: earning a living, sexual intercourse, having and raising children, and so on. Yet in Christian marriage each of these natural elements now participates in the power of Christ's cross and resurrection. This is what St. Thomas means when he says, "grace does not destroy, but perfects nature" (1, q.1, a.8, ad 2). When we distinguish between the moral virtue perfecting our nature and the theological virtues perfecting the life of grace in us, we must recognize that for the Christian the moral virtues themselves are gifts from God.

St. Thomas divides the moral virtues, which perfect the will, into the four cardinal virtues: temperance (self-control), prudence (practical wisdom), justice, and courage (fortitude). The Bible shows how the cardinal virtues are sent us from the wisdom of God and are intrinsically connected with each other: "If anyone loves righteousness, [wisdom's] labors are virtues; for she teaches self-control and prudence, justice and courage; nothing in life is more profitable for men than these" (Wis 8:7). Insofar as these virtues are gifts from God, they are called *infused* moral virtues; insofar as they are learned by upbringing and practice, they are called *acquired* moral virtues. Within the life of grace, the infused moral virtues allow the person to love God and to love neighbor, and display the reality that grace leaves no aspect of our lives untransformed. The acquired moral virtues, however, are not irrelevant. They allow the person with the infused moral virtues to act with a greater ease and alacrity, or readiness. The moral virtues as whole can be viewed as those good habits that allow us to act justly with ourselves, with those near to us, and with our wider society.

As we have noted, however, God alone will make us happy. The theological virtues of faith, hope, and love (charity) provide for intimate union with God. St. Thomas calls these virtues "theological" because they cannot be separated from God (*theos* in the Greek). The theological virtues come to us from God. St. Paul emphasizes this when he writes, "God's love has been poured into our hearts through the Holy Spirit who has been given to us" (Rom 5:5). God reveals to us the theological virtues of faith, hope, and love, and they direct our actions to God as our ultimate end: "For the love of Christ controls us" (2 Cor 5:14). The theological virtues presuppose humility. St. Thomas teaches, "Our Lord himself wished us to be conformed to him, chiefly in humility and meekness, according to Mt 11:29, 'Learn of Me, because I am meek and humble of heart,' and in charity, according to Jn 15:12, 'Love one another, as I have loved you'" (1-2, q.68, a.1). Although the list of the theological virtues (faith, hope, and charity) does not include humility, the virtue of humility shapes the whole Christian moral life. In humility, the Christian virtues are not earned, but received as gifts.

The moral and the theological virtues give us the power to be in relationship to God. As St. John writes, "to all who received him, who believed in his name, he gave power to become children of God" (Jn 1:12). Since God is the ultimate reality, we could also say that the virtues allow us to embrace reality instead of hiding from it. But God's gifts do not stop with the virtues. The action of the Holy Spirit in the hearts of the faithful extends to the specific gifts of the Spirit.

St. Thomas identifies the gifts of the Holy Spirit as enumerated in Isaiah 11:2–3: "the Spirit of the Lord shall rest upon him, the spirit of wisdom and understanding, the spirit of counsel and might, the spirit of knowledge and the fear of the Lord. And his delight shall be in the fear of the Lord." In the Vulgate translation of the Bible used by St. Thomas, the first "fear of the Lord" read as "piety." He thus enumerates the seven gifts as follows: wisdom, understanding, counsel, fortitude, knowledge, piety, and fear. The gifts of the Spirit allow us to be receptive to the motions of the Spirit in our souls. To attain happiness with God we need to be guided by God himself. St. Thomas writes, "the gifts of the Holy Spirit are habits whereby man is perfected to obey readily the Holy Spirit" (1-2, q.68, a.3), which corresponds to Romans 8:14, "For all who are led by the Spirit of God are sons of God." The theological virtues and the gifts of the Holy Spirit work together to relate human beings in friendship with the Trinity.

The Christian moral life thus encompasses far more than merely following a set of rules or getting into a constrictive habitual routine. It is a life lived "in Christ," a life of "the glorious liberty of the children of God" (Rom 8:21). It is very much the life of one led by the Spirit. The Holy Spirit inspires within our souls the virtuous "habits" that enable us to act freely to embrace the truth in love, to become people of justice.

It should not be thought that this emphasis on the virtues and gifts of the Holy Spirit undercuts the divine commandments, which are guidelines for justice. Indeed, apart from obedience to God's commandments, the moral life is unthinkable. As the book of Ecclesiastes eloquently puts it, "The end of the matter; all has been heard. Fear God, and keep his commandments; for this is the whole duty of man" (Eccles 12:13). To obey the commandments, however, we need to have the capacity to do so. On one level, the virtues give us the power to keep the commandments. The goal of the virtues is to perfect us in order to attain happiness with God. The goal of the commandments is to guide us along the same path. The virtues and the commandments complement each other in the quest for happiness, animated by the Holy Spirit.

The Two Freedoms

It is worth noting that some people chafe at the notion that true freedom comes in submitting ourselves to God. Happiness, according to this view, is found in having the freedom to choose whatever one wants. In this light, freedom and morality would be *competitors* for the human spirit. This view of freedom, however, lacks the fullness of freedom. It is freedom of indifference—a freedom from interference. A higher form of freedom exists. It is freedom to achieve the good—a freedom for excellence. Although these two different freedoms are not often distinguished, anyone can quickly recognize the reality of the distinction. If someone asks me, "Am I free to play the piano?" I can answer in two ways: "Yes, it's my piano, I am free to play it whenever I want. I am free to hit it with a sledge hammer as a matter of fact"; or "Yes, I can play any song you want since I have been playing the piano for twenty years now." The first "yes" answer expresses the freedom from interference; the second "yes" answer reveals the freedom for excellence.

Any consideration of freedom and morality must be clear about what kind of freedom is involved. Virtues may well conflict with a freedom from interference. Virtues make it possible, however, for us to have the freedom for excellence. Apart from the skill of playing the piano, a person lacks the freedom to play. Apart from the virtues, a person lacks the freedom to choose the good. The person may occasionally do good things, but cannot be counted on reliably to do so.

As St. Thomas recognizes, the two kinds of freedoms complement each other. In order to have freedom for human excellence, we need to have some amount of freedom from interference. Persons restricted from choosing freely to do right or wrong are prevented from acting as free persons. Any attempts by parents or governments to prevent all wrongdoing will invariably make those under their authority incapable of acting rightly as well. But if freedom from interference is raised up as the standard by which we judge things right or wrong, it quickly becomes nonsensical. Complete freedom from interference—no laws against murder, child abuse, and so on—is obviously not desirable. No one would deny, however, that complete freedom for excellence is a good thing. There is no limit that need be placed upon a person's realization of such freedom. This leads us to conclude that freedom for excellence is the true notion of freedom under which falls the valid, yet partial, notion of freedom from interference.

The Fullness of the Christian Life: The Theological Virtues

The study of the moral life must move beyond the general category of virtue to the particular virtues. Since the theological virtues join the person to God, they are more important than the moral virtues. Faith, hope, and charity (love) take precedence over the cardinal virtues of temperance, prudence, courage, and justice. Associated with each virtue (except temperance) is a gift of the Holy Spirit. Through the conjunction of the virtues and the gifts, the Christian moral life describes the dynamic process of our divinization.

The Christian Virtues and the Corresponding Gifts of the Holy Spirit

Faith	Understanding and Knowledge
Hope	Fear of the Lord
Charity	Wisdom
Prudence	Counsel
Justice	Piety
Courage	Fortitude
Temperance	Fear of the Lord

The theological virtue of faith is life-changing. It is the real beginning of eternal life, the initiation of our friendship with the triune God by means of a new knowing of God, given us by God himself. It is not an abstract openness to the unknown, or a mere trust that God exists. While the theological virtues of hope and charity perfect the will, faith perfects the intellect. As a theological virtue, faith is faith in God by intellectual assent to what he has revealed through the Church. Since God has revealed *divine* mysteries, these truths lie beyond the demonstrative power of our natural intellect. We need the supernatural virtue of faith, a gift of grace, to assent to the revealed truths—to judge with certitude that what God has revealed is true, that is, reveals the highest truth about reality or being.

But how do we know what God has revealed? God is not only the content of faith, but also the giver of faith. God himself inspires us to assent to the fullness of truth "as proposed to us in the Scriptures, according to the teaching of the Church which has the right understanding of them" (2-2, q.5, a.3, ad 2). As such, faith requires assent to all of the teachings of the Church, since the assent is to *God revealing*. Faith is not a private matter, unrelated to the community God has formed or to our lives in the world. It belongs to the assent of faith to confess our faith in the public gathering of the Church. Moreover, although the act of faith includes assenting to many statements about God, it is crucial to see that it does not rest in those statements but in God himself. When a person believes what God has revealed, the person *believes God* and inaugurates a new friendship that reorders all our other relationships. This intellectual assent is only possible with a movement of the will toward God, moving the intellect's assent. Along with the virtue of faith go the Holy Spirit's gift of understanding, which penetrates into the mysteries of faith, and gift of knowledge, which discerns what is to be believed.

Hope is the theological virtue by which we desire eternal life and are confident of attaining it with God's assistance. On the natural level hope is the desire to attain a difficult good. But the ultimate good of human life is the enjoyment of God in eternal life. This is a difficult good indeed, and would be impossible if God had left us to the powers proper to our nature. Faith reveals, however, that God's power knows no limits and that "the Lord is merciful and gracious, slow to anger and abounding in steadfast love" (Ps 103:8). We cannot attain heaven on our own; God must assist us. Hope thus leads to confidence in attaining heaven since the one who assists us is omnipotent and merciful. As the author of Hebrews writes, "Let us hold fast the confession of our hope without wavering, for he who promised is faithful" (Heb 10:23). Together with hope belongs the Holy Spirit's gift of fear of the Lord. Not the fear of a servant, this is the fear of children who fear offending their beloved father.

The importance of hope shines more brightly when we recall a significant aspect of our life that remains despite our growth in the virtues—namely, sin and vice. As 1 John 1:8 teaches, "If we say we have no sin, we deceive ourselves, and the truth is not in us." Once the perfection associated with the virtues is glimpsed, the reflective person might well despair of ever attaining it. The first thing we find when we attempt to practice the Christian virtues is that we fail. Hope thus forms an anchor in our lives. Because we are included in the new covenant of Jesus Christ, his promises and his merits ground our confidence in attaining heaven. We cooperate through repentance and confession of our sins, frequent recourse to the sacraments and prayer, and the daily effort to begin again. As we saw in the previous chapter on providence, the fact that our salvation depends entirely on God does not exclude the role of our free will. It is our work *and* God's work, as we have seen in Philippians 2:12–13: "work out your own salvation with fear and trembling; for God is at work in you, both to will and to work for his good pleasure."

At special occasions such as weddings, Christians often are reminded, "Faith, hope, love abide, these three; but the greatest of these is love" (1 Cor 13:13). Indeed, the supernatural virtue of love, or charity, is the center of the Christian life. As St. Paul says, "if I have all faith, so as to remove mountains, but have not love, I am nothing" (1 Cor 13:2). Charity is the only one of the three theological virtues that remains in heaven. St. Thomas defines charity simply as *friendship with God*. As Jesus tells his disciples, "No longer do I call you servants, for the servant does not know what his master is doing; but I have called you friends, for all that I have heard from my Father I have made known to you" (Jn 15:15).

As this passage suggests, friendship requires a kind of equity among the partners. How then can we be *friends* of God, who infinitely transcends creatures? God makes us his friends by healing and elevating our nature so that it shares in his nature, his divine knowing and loving. Once the image of God is restored in us, we possess a likeness to God. Charity is the most excellent of all of the virtues since it alone loves God for who he is and not, as with hope, for what he can do for us. As St. Thomas expresses it, "charity attains God himself that it may rest in him, but not that something may accrue to us from him" (2-2, q.23, a.6). With charity our hearts find their rest in God.

St. Thomas teaches that charity is the "form" of all of the other virtues. The charitable person performs all actions for the love of God. Thus, charity, as a "form" or pattern, guides all the virtues to their proper end. What happens when charity does not form the other virtues? Faith, for instance, could exist in someone without love. As St. James teaches, "Even the demons believe—and shudder" (Jas 2:19). This would be faith unformed by charity. Faith formed by charity not only knows God and what he has revealed, but also loves the God thus known. Charity forms the cardinal virtues—prudence, justice, courage, temperance—as well. Charity, for instance, orders temperance so that instead of fasting to lose weight, it becomes possible to fast for love of God. Human beings attain the goal of heaven by means of actions informed by charity. Along with the virtue of charity, the Holy Spirit gives the gift of wisdom. Wisdom allows the person "to judge all things according to the divine truth" (2-2, q.45, a.1, ad 2). It is the wisdom spoken of by St. James: "the wisdom from above is first pure, then peaceable, gentle, open to reason, full of mercy and good fruits, without uncertainty or insincerity" (Jas 3:17).

The Fullness of the Christian Life: The Moral Virtues

The first moral virtue to be considered is prudence, or practical wisdom, or sound judgment. The word "prudence" today is associated with excessive caution. The virtue of prudence, however, has no special fondness for caution; rather it describes the habit of acting decisively. Prudence does not choose the end, but selects the means to attain it. St. Augustine defines prudence as "the knowledge of what to seek and what to avoid" (*Eighty-Three Questions*, q.61). Aristotle says that "prudence is right reason in action" (*Nicomachean Ethics* 6, 5). The prudent person sizes up the situation and then chooses the best course of action. This may take time or it may be instantaneous. In the case of deciding whether to marry someone, prudence may well take its time to gain experience of the person's character. In the case of rescuing children from a burning building, prudence chooses quickly which door to enter.

Prudence not only includes making the right decision, but also demands that we carry out the decision. In this way prudence links the intellectual and moral virtues (knowing and doing). Prudence, moreover, shapes the other moral virtues insofar as it enables the just person to act justly, the courageous person to act bravely, and the temperate person to act with self-control. St. Thomas suggests that along with the virtue of prudence comes the gift of counsel. Through the gift of counsel, the Holy Spirit directs the mind to gain insight into the given situation in order to act in the best possible way.

Justice concerns a person's relationships with others. St. Thomas defines justice as giving others their due. In contrast to the contemporary view of justice that insists on treating everyone equally, the virtue of justice gives others what is *due* them. For example, it is an act of justice for a father to spend more time with his children than with the children of strangers. Likewise, a just society will devote more resources to the care of mentally and physically handicapped children, who need extra resources, than to children without these handicaps. The greatest "other" who is due something from us is God. Justice thus includes the virtue of religion whereby we give to God the worship that is due him; religion, as an act of justice, is natural to the human creature. The Holy Spirit's gift of piety gives us a filial affection toward God: as St. Paul writes, "you have received the spirit of sonship. When we cry, 'Abba! Father!' it is the Spirit himself bearing witness with our spirit that we are children of God" (Rom 8:15–16).

Courage and temperance concern the guidance of the passions by reason. In contrast to the ancient Stoic philosophers, St. Thomas holds that our passions are not beyond the bounds of our reason, as if the best we could do was to control or dominate our unruly passions. Rather, the unity of soul and body is such that our rational soul can inform every aspect of our human personality. In this light, the virtue of courage, or fortitude, is the habit by which our *reason* governs well the irascible appetite, that is, the emotions for resisting evil and overcoming difficulty. Courage is classically defined as the willingness to fall in battle; yet in the Christian life, the greatest expression of courage is the willingness to be a martyr for Christ. The courageous person makes proper use of the God-given emotion of anger to pounce upon evil. Moreover, the courageous person shows patience and endurance of evil. Patience is more than simply the willingness to endure evil; patience accepts the difficulty joyfully without becoming excessively saddened. The virtue of courage is complemented with a gift of the Holy Spirit of the same name. This pairing of a virtue with a gift of the Holy Spirit again shows that as the infused virtue perfects the human soul, there also needs to be the immediate direction of the Holy Spirit in order for us to live well. God is present transforming and guiding our bodily passions through the grace of the Holy Spirit in our soul.

Temperance, or temperateness, regulates our desire for sensible goods (the concupiscible appetite). For this reason, temperance is above all associated with moderation in food, drink, and sex. Temperance does not, however, necessarily mean abstinence. For instance, the Benedictine Rule was not for teetotalers; St. Benedict instructed each monk to have one glass of wine per day. The temperate person is not one who feels no desire. Instead, the emotions and desires are brought under the gentle guidance of reason. A temperate husband on his wedding night will arouse great desire for his bride. The husband's virtue of temperance, however, assures that his desire will not grow so great as to blind the groom to the inherent dignity of his bride; she must ever be loved as a *person* to be served and never as an *object* for his own gratification.

In the case of resistance to evils, it is more common to fail by fleeing from them. The virtue of fortitude thus strengthens our capacity to stand firm when confronted with the difficult aspects of reality. For instance, fortitude allows a mother to carry to full term a child diagnosed with a terminal illness. In the case of our desire for material pleasure, however, most fail by desiring them inordinately. Temperateness guides our desires for sensible pleasures so that they will not lead to our own physical and/or spiritual destruction. The virtue of temperance plays a pivotal role in the reversal of the original sin of Adam and Eve. Recall that, in the narrative of the Fall, Eve disobeyed the commandment of God when "she saw that the tree was good for food, and that it was a delight to the eyes, and that the tree was to be desired to make one wise" (Gen 3:6). The good things of God's creation will only satisfy when we *first* cling to the One who created them.

St. Thomas discusses the virtue of humility and the vice of pride within the context of temperance. The battle between pride and humility forms the fundamental drama within human history. Pride is the ultimate kind of intemperance since it blinds one to the true reality of created things and instead only values them as they give pleasure to the self. The love of self becomes the standard by which to judge everything. Intemperance has greater ramifications than mere sensual indulgence. At its root, the intemperate person seeks to replace God and his providential order of things with the order of value flowing from the person's own turbulent desires. Humility is a species of temperance because it reverses the destructive character of pride. The humble person recognizes that the universe is God's and that the person's desires must correspond to reality. St. Teresa of Avila concisely stated that humility is truth. Only the temperate person can set aside the false reality created by the love of self and embrace the true reality in which God is loved as the center of everything.

St. Thomas recognizes that an understanding of the virtues actually allows us to understand the world of the New Testament. As 2 Peter 1:4–5 states, God, in Christ, has promised to enable us "to become partakers of the divine nature. For this very reason make every effort to supplement your faith with virtue, and virtue with knowledge, and knowledge with self-control, and self-control with steadfastness, and steadfastness with godliness, and godliness with brotherly affection, and brotherly affection with love." Faith, although the foundation of the Christian life, needs to be supplemented with other virtues. God has adopted us as his children in Jesus Christ; and just as children share the same nature as their father, we are to become, in holiness, *like God*. Jesus himself commanded us, "Be perfect as your heavenly Father is perfect" (Mt 5:48; cf. Lev 19:2).

CHAPTER FOUR

LAW AND GRACE

Christian theologians like to ponder the strangeness of the human condition. We are created for a purpose, namely life with God, that we cannot reach by our own resources. In contrast, a rock can do all that it is meant to do from the mere fact of its being a rock. A rock is a rock because God created it; no further gift is required for the rock to be fully rock. Human beings, however, cannot be fully human in the way God intended, apart from further assistance from God, because human destiny is life with the Trinity. To add to the problem, human beings separated themselves from God by the sin of pride. The image of God in us needs to be healed and restored. The Psalmist speaks to this with particular tenderness, no doubt evoking tears in some of his listeners: "As a hart longs for flowing streams, so longs my soul for thee, O God. My soul thirsts for God, for the living God. When shall I come and behold the face of God?" (Ps 42:1–2).

Law and Grace

God helps us in two main ways: law and grace. Both law and grace are God's actions on us that lead us to find fulfillment, the true happiness that the Psalmist longs for. "Law" and "grace" are common words, but in Christian theology they have complex meanings. St. Thomas uses the term "law" in an analogous way: law principally refers to something in the real order of being, not to a mental construction. "Grace" can signify either God's free will to give us a share in the divine life, or the gift infused by God in the person's soul that makes the person a new creation. In the former sense, grace is the action of the Holy Spirit; in the latter sense, grace is an effect in the creature who now shares in the divine life. Law and grace provide the context that makes the virtuous life possible. They are the two ways, the right and left hands, so to speak, by which God moves us to return to him.

We have seen that when God creates things, he has the whole of their existence in mind. This whole existence includes what they are (their origin), what they are meant to become (their goal), and how they are to move from what they are to what they are meant to be (their pattern of fulfillment). If we consider the truth that God's eternity embraces each moment of time and that God's infinity embraces each point in space, then we glimpse the mystery that God's knowledge embraces each moment and each point of his creation. As the Psalmist expresses it, "Whither shall I go from thy Spirit? Or whither shall I flee from thy presence? If I ascend to heaven, thou art there! If I make my bed in Sheol, thou art there! If I take the wings of the morning and dwell in the uttermost parts of the sea, even there thy hand shall lead me, and thy right hand shall hold me." (Ps 139:7–10). God is present in all parts of his creation; he continually acts to sustain and to perfect his creation.

Divine providence extends to all of creation, but especially to humans. God's providence orders us to our end principally by means of law and grace. Since God is the one who created us, he alone can work to bring us to our perfection. To speak of God bringing us to our perfection might suggest some kind of conflict with human freedom. God's action of providence, however, does not violate our free will since God's providence is the source of our free will. As the source of our free will, God's will exists in a noncompetitive relationship with our will. Apart from God's creative and providential action, we would not even possess free will.

Divine providence forms the context of a proper discussion of law and grace. Once viewed in this context, law does not restrict human fulfillment; law instead enables human fulfillment. In the modern world, law typically comes into play when the exercise of one person's freedom conflicts with another person's. Law, according to this view, restricts my freedom so that others may have freedom. If human law exists merely as a restraint of our freedom, then divine law can appear as an opposition to our freedom. According to this view of law, divine law restricts our freedom for the sake of something greater, perhaps in this case eternal life. Divine law thus appears arbitrary.

In fact, far from being restrictive, God's law is the expression of divine Wisdom, directing things toward their end (1-2, q.90, a.1). God's law is not voluntaristic or arbitrary. Rather, as St. Thomas notes, divine law is the wise order of creation. Our freedom blossoms by following the law. For example, a man who jumps from a ten-story building to break the law of gravity does not break the law, but himself gets broken. The man's fall simply demonstrates the law of gravity. A man who breaks God's law does not break God, but himself gets broken. Thus the Book of Judges, after telling of a horrifying rape, mutilation, and the resulting civil war, concludes pointedly, "In those days there was no king in Israel; every man did what was right in his own eyes" (Judg 21:25). In fact, our lives—when seen in their ultimate reality—demonstrate God's law.

Law and Order

St. Thomas distinguishes five kinds of law: eternal law, natural law, human law, and divine law, which includes both the old law and the new law. What unites these diverse kinds of "law"? All law is rational, since it flows from an intelligent lawgiver, either God or man. All law is ordered not simply to the good of each individual, but to the common good of the community. Law can only be given by those who have the capacity to govern the community. Eternal law, for instance, is God's ordering of the cosmos. Human law is the governing authority's order of a political community. Although we use the same term, "law," it is obvious that the various levels of law are quite different as well.

Eternal law is another name for divine providence. It is the way God orders the universe and leads everything in the universe to reach its end. As St. Thomas writes, "God imprints on the whole of nature the principles of its proper actions" (1-2, q.93, a.5). Creation itself exists only as a gift of God: "In his hand are the depths of the earth; the heights of the mountains are his also. The sea is his, for he made it; for his hands formed the dry land" (Ps 95:4–5).

Within the context of the eternal law, we come to the much-discussed reality of natural law. In his Letter to the Romans, St. Paul says that when the Gentiles act rightly, "they show that what the law requires is written on their hearts" (2:15). God has given to each created thing some innate ability to fulfill its purpose, and the human creature is no exception. Even the Gentiles who were not yet part of God's covenant had a law "written on their hearts." This is called the natural law. St. Thomas succinctly describes the natural law as "the rational creature's participation in the eternal law" (1-2, q.91, a.2). As rational creatures—that is, as creatures who participate by our rational powers in the eternal law—we possess certain inclinations to the good and certain first principles of right action. St. Thomas explains that "the precepts of the natural law are to the practical reason, what the first principles of demonstrations [such as the principle of non-contradiction] are to the speculative reason; because both are self-evident principles" (1-2, q.94, a.2). By using our reason and free will, we share in the exercise of God's providence.

The natural law provides a common moral feature to human beings of diverse cultures. The precepts, or principles, of the natural law flow from the inclinations proper to our nature. The human will has a natural inclination to desire what is good. The first precept of the natural law, therefore, is that *good is to be done and sought after, and evil is to be avoided.* This basic principle is shown even when many human beings do not choose what is good. A person who has done something evil almost always offers some kind of excuse or explanation trying to justify the wrong behavior, to try to make it look right or good. Even disagreements over moral questions express a fundamental agreement that good is to be done and evil avoided. If there were no standard of right and wrong, then it would be absurd for people to argue. Because of sin, the mere knowledge that good is to be done and evil to be avoided cannot act as a trustworthy guide for human action. For instance, in the debates over slavery before the Civil War, both sides appealed to standards of morality and argued that they were doing the good, even though now we recognize that the pro-slavery position was profoundly immoral.

Based on this first principle, St. Thomas notes that three other basic guidelines of the natural law follow, having to do in turn with the individual, the family, and the community. First, there is the inclination and obligation of the preservation of our own lives. Second, there is the stability of marriage as the sphere for sexual intercourse and for the raising of children. Third, there is an inclination to know the truth about God and to live in society and a corresponding obligation to seek the truth about God and to avoid contention with others. It is significant that questions about God belong to natural law in addition to being part of Christian revelation. Indeed, God and religion cannot be removed from public discourse without violating a basic precept of our human nature. In the political sphere human dignity requires that a person be free from religious coercion, but human dignity requires as well that the truth about God be proposed to him or her. The right to religious freedom goes along with a right to religious truth.

Human beings can recognize God—at least partially—from his creation. As St. Paul says, "Ever since the creation of the world [God's] invisible nature, namely, his eternal power and deity, has been clearly perceived in the things that have been made" (Rom 1:20). As important as the natural law in us is, however, it fails to lead us to our end in three significant areas. First, because of sin, the natural inclination to the good has been severely weakened and even replaced with an inclination to do evil—what St. Thomas, with the Christian tradition, calls concupiscence. St. Paul expresses the fallen condition of disordered desire: "For I do not do the good I want, but the evil I do not want is what I do. . . . I see in my members another law at war with the law of my mind and making me captive to the law of sin which dwells in my members" (Rom 7:19, 23). Not only has sin weakened our inclination to the good, sin has sickened our will in such as way that it cannot reliably choose the good. We may avoid sin in this or that particular action, but apart from the grace of God it is impossible to avoid sin in general. St. Thomas actually speaks of a habit or custom of sinning that obscures our perception of the natural law (1-2, q.98, a.6, ad 1). This custom of sinning refers both to the individual's knowledge and to the sensibilities of the wider culture.

Second, the natural law provides basic inclinations and precepts, but these are insufficient to guide human action in the concrete situations of human life. The basic inclinations and precepts need to be particularized both through human law and through the virtue of prudence. For instance, the natural law teaches us that we should preserve life. In the United States, human law specifies this by making it illegal to drive above a certain speed, such as 70 miles per hour. Prudence specifies this further by judging in a particular situation, such as a heavy downpour, that the standard speed limit itself is too high. The implications of the role of human law and prudence are manifold. If the human law in a particular country goes against the natural law, then many of its citizens may likewise be blinded to the true wickedness of certain actions. Consider the cases of the forced slavery of African Americans, of abortion, of euthanasia, and of the Holocaust. St. Thomas himself observed in the thirteenth century that some countries did not consider theft wrong. Natural law, however, can provide a way to judge human laws. If the laws of a government contradict the natural law, then they are not true laws and therefore do not require obedience. While civil disobedience may create doubt in general about the force of law, when the confusion of disobedience is outweighed by the evil of the law, civil disobedience should be used. An effective example of this is the civil disobedience during the civil rights movement in the 1950s and 1960s.

The final problem with the natural law does not concern our inability to follow it, but concerns its end or *telos*. The natural law aims at the perfection that is proper to our human nature. We have already seen, however, that the human creature has been created in grace. Creation in grace means that God, by the sheer gift of his grace, ordains that human beings have an end that is beyond their nature, namely, life as children of God. Just as human children share in the nature of their human parents, similarly, if we are to be children of God, then we must share in God's nature. Once this standard of human perfection was introduced into creation, it became simply impossible for the natural law to lead us to total happiness. The natural law requires that it be completed with the gift of the divine law by which God leads human beings to eternal life with him.

Divine law has two parts: the old law of Israel (that is, the Mosaic Law or Torah) and the new law of Jesus Christ. The corruption of human nature and the loss of the life of grace had a historical origin in sin. If the disease is historical, then the cure is played out in history as well. The whole of the divine law heals human nature and elevates it to live with God; just as human law aims at making us fit for human society, so divine law aims at making us fit for heaven. According to God's wisdom, the divine law accomplishes this salvation in stages, so that the salvation might truly be accomplished historically. The structure of the old law and the new law thus reveals the divine pedagogy, by which God leads his wayward children back to himself.

One Law, Old and New

The old law and the new law are connected intimately as two stages of one process of divine instruction. The term "old law" covers the whole of the Old Testament, referring specifically to the Mosaic Law as continued and expanded in the covenant under King David. The Mosaic Law—the Ten Commandments and associated particular laws—was good since it came from God. As St. Paul writes of the Mosaic Law, "the law is holy and the commandment is holy and just and good" (Rom 7:12). As a covenant between God and man, the Mosaic Law brought Israel into relationship with God and began the process of restoring the unity of man with God that had been lost through sin.

St. Thomas holds that the Mosaic Law structured the life of Israel in three main ways: the moral law, the ceremonial law, and the judicial law. The moral law as summarized in the Ten Commandments taught Israel how to live rightly. Although in principle these commandments could be known from the natural law, human beings needed God to reveal the commandments to them so they could know them without error and with confidence. The Ten Commandments therefore reveal the natural law to man. These commandments are rules that permanently govern human life. The ceremonial law orders Israel to the right worship of the true God. The animal sacrifices thus are both the renunciation of idolatry—since the pagan nations often worshipped gods in the form of animals—and the recognition that all things are received from God and are to be offered back to him. The judicial law structured the life of the political kingdom of Israel. This threefold division of the Mosaic Law provides the Christian Church, which *fulfills* rather than *negates* the Mosaic Law, with a clear rationale for retaining some of the commandments of Old Testament while eschewing others. The moral law is retained, though now within the context of Christ's love. In contrast, the ceremonial law is fulfilled and elevated in the greater ceremonies of the new covenant, and the political law is fulfilled and elevated in the Church's nature as the universal kingdom of God. This explains why there is no contradiction between upholding the book of Leviticus's prohibition of homosexual actions, as contrary to human nature, and dismissing the prohibition of eating pork, which relates exclusively to ceremonial purity.

Although the Mosaic Law was good and initiated the people of Israel into a covenantal relationship with God, St. Thomas points out that it remained incomplete or imperfect. It ordered people to God, but it did not instill within them the power to reach God. The people continually violate the covenant that God makes with them. Immediately after Israel enters into covenant with God at Mt. Sinai to become "a kingdom of priests and a holy nation" (Ex 19:6), Israel's first act of priesthood is to commit idolatry by worshipping the golden calf. King David commits adultery with Bathsheba and has her husband killed in battle immediately after receiving the promise from God that one of David's heirs will remain on the throne forever (2 Sam 7–11). This cycle of blessing and sin repeats itself throughout human history. Even today, although in Jesus Christ God's definitive blessing has been revealed, each of us continues stubbornly to reject God's blessing and suffer the wounds of sin (as witnessed by our continuing need for the sacrament of penance).

In the Old Testament, the history of human violation of God's covenants was used by God to show the depth of human sin. The prophets of Israel foretold that God would establish a *new covenant* that would finally overcome sin. We see this in Jeremiah 31:31–33: "Behold, the days are coming says the Lord, when I will make a new covenant with the house of Israel and the house of Judah. . . . I will put my law within them, and I will write it upon their hearts"; and in Ezekiel 36:26: "A new heart I will give you, and a new spirit I will put within you; and I will take out of your flesh the heart of stone and give you a heart of flesh. And I will put my spirit within you, and cause you to walk in my statutes and be careful to observe my ordinances." The Mosaic Law was good, but it was incomplete. Israel awaited a new covenant in which God's law would be written on their hearts, new hearts of flesh, hearts capable of full obedience.

This new covenant is inaugurated in Jesus Christ, who is God made man. In the new covenant, we can be incorporated into Christ—and thus be made into friends of God—through faith and baptism. St. Paul teaches, "The law was our custodian until Christ came, that we might be justified by faith. But now that faith has come, we are no longer under a custodian; for in Christ Jesus you are all sons of God, through faith. For as many of you as were baptized into Christ have put on Christ" (Gal 3:24–27). Faith and baptism enable us to enter into the new law by which we are restored in right relation to God. As St. John writes, "For the law was given through Moses; grace and truth come through Jesus Christ" (Jn 1:17).

Yet an astute reader may question why St. Thomas speaks of a new *law*. Does not the quote from John 1:17 suggest that the *law* is associated with the Old Testament and *grace* with the New? The New Testament, however, discusses the new law of grace in the two books most dedicated to showing that in Christ we are freed from observing the law of Moses: Galatians and Romans. Galatians 6:2 tells us, "Bear one another's burdens, and so fulfill the law of Christ." Christ has fulfilled the law not so that we are excused from the law, but so that we become capable of fulfilling it. This is Ezekiel's prophecy of the new heart of flesh capable of keeping

God's commandments. Romans 13:8 says the same: "He who loves his neighbor has fulfilled the law."

Both of these passages speak of loving one's neighbor and thus fulfilling the law. But how is such fulfillment possible? St. Paul explains, "For the law of the Spirit of life in Christ Jesus has set me free from the law of sin and death" (Rom 8:2). A new law—the law of the Spirit of life—has freed man from sin. St. Paul continues, "For God has done what the law, weakened by the flesh, could not do: sending his own Son in the likeness of sinful flesh and as a sin offering, he condemned sin in the flesh, in order that the just requirement of the law might be fulfilled in us, who walk not according to the flesh but according to the Spirit" (Rom 8:3–4). Again we see that the law is now "fulfilled in us." The law of the Spirit is called a law because it is meant to be the new principle of our lives: we should "walk according to the Spirit."

The new law, the law of the Spirit, and the law of Christ all signify this new reality of divine grace acting in the believer. St. Thomas states that the new law first of all signifies the grace of the Holy Spirit. Since the new law is the grace of the Holy Spirit, the new law can do what the natural law could not. It can lead us to our supernatural end of life with God both through the forgiveness of our sins through Jesus Christ (Lk 24:47) and through the elevation of our nature to become children of God (Jn 1:12).

In a secondary sense, the new law refers to something tangible. It is both the gift of the sacraments and the entire inspired text of the New Testament. The sacraments communicate the grace of God to us and the New Testament instructs us how to use well his grace. The new law forms the oral and written apostolic tradition, instructing the faithful what to believe and how to live. In St. Thomas's view, the greatest and most concise written expression of the new law is Jesus' Sermon on the Mount. Jesus simultaneously intensifies the law and fulfills it: "Think not that I have come to abolish the law and the prophets; I have come not to abolish them but to fulfill them" (Mt 5:17).

The Sermon on the Mount, however, should be read not as a list of imperatives but rather as a light for giving glory to God through good works. As Jesus teaches, "Let your light so shine before men, that they may see your good works and give glory to your Father who is in heaven" (Mt 5:16). St. Augustine describes the Sermon as a "perfect pattern of the Christian life" (*On the Lord's Sermon on the Mount*). Yet the written expression of the new law should not obscure the deeper spiritual reality of the new law as the grace of the Holy Spirit. No longer is the good life summarized in the Greek dictum "Know yourself." Christ now expresses the moral life in the invitation to "be perfect, as your heavenly Father is perfect" (Mt 5:48). The new law constitutes a new horizon of the moral life as the graced life of children of God. According to St. Thomas, the new law is the most perfect state of life possible in this *present* life (1-2, q.106, a.4). As the Mosaic Law prefigures the new law, so the new law prefigures the final state of glory in heaven.

The Life of Grace

What is grace? Grace, in us, can be described in different ways. It is the gift of divine sonship (divine filiation): "But to all who received [the Word], who believed in his name, he gave power to become children of God" (Jn 1:12). Grace can also be seen as the indwelling of the Holy Trinity in the hearts of the faithful: "Jesus answered him, 'If a man loves me, he will keep my word, and my Father will love him, and we will come to him and make our home with him'" (Jn 14:23). Grace, as God's indwelling in us, indicates a radically new relationship with God that goes far beyond his presence in us as creator and sustainer of our being. This new presence is called *sanctifying grace* because it makes the recipient holy. All of these descriptions of grace emphasize that when we are speaking of grace, we are describing not a "thing," but a new relationship with God.

Grace operates as a new principle of life. Just as the natural gifts of reason and will enable a person to know, to live, and to act in the world, the supernatural gift of grace enables a person to know, to live, and to act in intimate union with God. It is common, therefore, to distinguish between the light of reason and the light of grace. This distinction allows us to see how grace, which transforms the essence of the soul (the image of God), is the foundation for all of the Christian virtues that perfect the powers of the soul. In the case of acquired virtues, the light of reason provides the capacity for rational action. The acquired virtues perfect and hone this natural capacity. In the case of the virtues infused by God, such as faith, hope, and love, the light of grace provides the capacity for supernatural action. The infused virtues are gifts from God to perfect and hone this new capacity.

Although the light of grace is one, it has diverse manifestations. St. Thomas makes several important distinctions in his discussion of grace. First, there is the distinction between operative and cooperative grace. Operative grace is when God acts in us *without* us. Since we were dead in our sins, as St. Paul says, we were incapable of doing anything to restore our relationship with God. The initial act of our justification is entirely a free gift from God through Jesus Christ. Because of the weakness of our wills, we cannot even cooperate in the first turning back to God. This operative grace is offered to everyone: "Jesus stood up and proclaimed, 'If any one thirst, let him come to me and drink. He who believes in me, as the scripture has said, "Out of his heart shall flow rivers of living water."' Now this he said about the Spirit, which those who believed in him were to receive" (Jn 7:37–39). Cooperative grace then allows us to respond to God's invitation. Thus even our cooperation and response to God's initiative is a gift of grace as well.

Another important distinction is observed between habitual grace and actual grace. Habitual grace constitutes the prime meaning of grace: our possession of the habit, or the skill, of living in right relation with God. It signals that the new relationship with God given by grace has a certain permanence and stability; it is not something destroyed by the first breath of wind. The notion that grace is something habitual in us—giving us new powers for acting—is what is meant by the phrase "being in a state of grace." Habitual grace is given in baptism and lost only through mortal sin. Once lost, repentance and confession are necessary to restore it. But just as the fitness of our physical body will wax or wane depending on our activity, so will habitual grace wax or wane depending on our actions. Venial sins weaken our wills and make us more likely to lose habitual grace. Actual grace, St. Thomas notes, is especially how the human will is "prepared for the gift of habitual grace itself" (1-2, q.109, a.6). The Holy Spirit inwardly prompts and assists the person's movement toward the new relationship with God through Jesus Christ. Actual grace increases through prayer, devout reception of the sacraments, and the spiritual and corporal works of mercy.

A final distinction of grace is between sanctifying grace (*gratia gratum faciens*) and gratuitous grace (*gratia gratis data*). Sanctifying grace is what its name suggests—grace that makes the recipient holy. Gratuitous grace is grace freely given to us for the sake of making other people holy. Sanctifying grace unites the faithful to their ultimate end, whereas gratuitous grace—the ability to prophesy, perform miracles, convert sinners, and so forth—serves simply to dispose people to be united to their ultimate end; thus in the Gospels, many people see miracles but do not believe. For this reason, sanctifying grace, although it may not show itself in signs and wonders, is of greater dignity than gratuitous grace.

The two greatest effects of God's grace are the initial justification of the sinner (the effect of operative grace) and human merit (the effect of co-operative grace). The justification of the sinner is completely the gift of God. It requires a movement of the will by which the person chooses to love God and to detest sin. Because of the damaging effects of sin, our free will cannot cooperate in the initial turning toward God. This is indicated by St. Paul and St. John: "God shows his love for us in that while we were yet sinners Christ died for us" (Rom 5:8), and "In this is love, not that we loved God but that he loved us and sent his Son to be the expiation for our sins" (1 Jn 4:10). According to the New Testament, God alone initiates our salvation. In the fifth century, the Pelagian heresy contended that we contribute something to the initial act of justification. The Church, through St. Augustine and the Council of Carthage, rejected this view since it made Christ's Incarnation, death, and resurrection unnecessary. As St. Paul teaches, "if justification were through the law, then Christ died to no purpose" (Gal 2:21). By justification, the person is moved from a state of sin into a state of grace. The person moves from being a child of Adam to being a child of God.

St. Thomas holds that the movement initiating the person into life as a child of God enables the person to cooperate with this movement by performing actions pleasing to God. In this lies the notion of merit. Protestants have typically rejected any mention of merit, since it suggests to them that human beings can earn their salvation. The New Testament, however, speaks of a reward for our works. St. Paul teaches, "If the work which any man has built on the foundation survives, he will receive a reward" (1 Cor 3:14). Jesus says, "whoever gives to one of these little ones even a cup of cold water because he is a disciple, truly, I say to you, he shall not lose his reward" (Mt 10:42). No creature can merit anything from the Creator by means of its natural powers. When the Creator, however, lifts us up to share in his dignity, then we can perform actions worthy of reward even though God is performing those actions through us. As St. Paul writes, "it is no longer I who live, but Christ who lives in me" (Gal 2:20). As children of Adam, we can merit nothing before God; as God's own children, "partakers in the divine nature," we can. The sinner therefore in no way can merit the first gift of grace. Meritorious works do not compete with grace, but instead confirm the power of grace: as St. Augustine put it, "God crowns his gifts as our merits."

Although grace resides in individuals, it should not be understood in an individualistic way. Christians receive grace only as members of Christ's Mystical Body. The grace members receive comes from the grace of Christ as the Head of the Body. Grace is not our independent possession, but the lifeblood of the whole Christ, head and members. When St. Paul says to the members of the church at Corinth that "you are God's temple," he is addressing the Church as a whole and not the individual Christian (1 Cor 3:16). The Holy Spirit dwells within each member, but only insofar as the member is connected to the body. This same idea is preached by Jesus: "I am the vine, you are the branches. He who abides in me, and I in him, he it is that bears much fruit, for apart from me you can do nothing" (Jn 15:5). God does not direct his salvation merely to individuals. God's salvation brings individuals into unity, by adopting God's rebellious children into his divine family. Grace describes our movement from being isolated sinners to being adopted children, in the Son (Jesus Christ) and through the Holy Spirit, of one divine Father.

Christ the Teacher of the New Law of Grace

In the Gospel of Matthew, Jesus instructs his disciples, "Neither be called masters [teachers], for you have one master [teacher], the Christ" (Mt 23:10). All other teachers in the Church serve at best as Christ's representatives (see 1 Cor 4). It is hardly surprising that one of the greatest teachers in the Christian tradition, St. Thomas, presents Christ as the greatest teacher. We should begin by specifying the conception of teaching that will guide our discussion of Christ as the teacher of the new law of grace.

Teachers generally possess tools that make it possible for them to be good teachers. Classroom teachers, for example, often use blackboards and overhead projectors to stimulate the visual senses in addition to the auditory senses. The best teachers, however, do more than communicate information. They model a way of life so that students can navigate on their own the path laid before them. Teaching thus opens up new possibilities in the learner hitherto unnoticed or unrealized. With successful teaching, the student perfects these possibilities and comes to act upon them freely. Teaching communicates a way of life or a new ability for action. If this is true with mere human teachers, what new way of life will a teacher who is both God and man communicate?

Christ exercises an unparalleled teaching office since he not only teaches what needs to be done, but actually communicates the power to do it. The new way of life that he communicates is the new law of grace. Christ teaches by sending the Holy Spirit into the hearts of the faithful: "When the Counselor comes, whom I shall send to you from the Father, even the Spirit of truth, who proceeds from the Father, he will bear witness to me" (Jn 15:26). St. Thomas says that Christ, as the most excellent of teachers, "impresses his teaching on the hearts of his listeners" (3, q.42, a.4). This mention of hearts recalls the aforementioned prophecies of Jeremiah and Ezekiel regarding a new heart.

The perfect law—the new law of grace—requires the perfect teacher. The New Testament states that the old law was given to Moses through the ministry of angels (cf. Heb 2:2; Gal 3:19). In contrast, "in these last days he has spoken to us by a Son, whom he appointed the heir of all things, through whom also he created the world" (Heb 1:2). The excellence of the new covenant is demonstrated because it is given directly by God the Son. The new covenant is more powerful to forgive sin and to elevate human nature. The new law of grace is handed on by a teacher who is not merely human but also divine.

To speak of Christ as the teacher of the new law thus differs greatly from liberal strands of Christianity that seek to reduce Christ to a mere moral teacher. Since the Enlightenment, some philosophers and theologians, such as John Locke and Gotthold Lessing, have tried to retain the view of Christ as a great moral teacher while dispensing with faith in Christ as fully God and fully man (*perfectus Deus, perfectus homo*). If Christ were merely a human teacher, however, he would be utterly incapable of releasing the vise of sin through his teaching. The problem with the human race lies less in ignorance of what ought to be done, and more in the inclination to do what ought not to be done. Only if Christ is God can his teaching free us from sin and elevate us to share in the divine life.

The New Testament reveals that the whole of the moral life is ultimately the imitation of Christ. The language of virtue and law, of vice and sin, can only be understood in the context of the new law of grace communicated to us by Christ. The virtue of faith, for example, leads us to see that Christ is the one who makes faith possible. St. Thomas explicitly speaks of Christ as teacher in the treatment of faith: "Christ is the first and principal teacher (*doctor*) of spiritual teaching (*doctrina*) and faith" (2-2, q.7, a.7). Most habits or skills are learned when we place ourselves under teachers who possess the skills we desire and the ability to foster those skills in us. All of our own efforts plus the wisdom of the teacher, however, cannot make up for certain physical or mental defects we inevitably have. By contrast, Christ is the teacher *par excellence,* who in teaching the new law of grace not only guides us and forms us, but even re-creates us in his image. The Christian virtues must be learned by placing ourselves under Christ as our one teacher.

CHAPTER FIVE

JESUS CHRIST

Jesus said, "I am the way, and the truth, and the life" (Jn 14:6). He presents us with the way to live in order to achieve happiness by revealing to us the truth about God and humankind. When he invites us to dare to follow him, he tells us, "The water that I shall give him will become in him a spring of water welling up to eternal life" (Jn 4:14). Since Jesus communicates his own divine life to his followers, St. Thomas can state that "Christ as man is our way back to God" (1, q.2, prologue). Yet it is difficult to understand who Jesus Christ is. A college-educated friend of ours, having gone to church for years, mentioned one day in passing that although he admired his preacher as a person, he did not believe the preacher when he spoke of Jesus' divinity, since the preacher seemed to think that Jesus created the world. Since Jesus was born two thousand years ago, our friend explained, this seemed too far-fetched. When we explained about Jesus being fully God and fully man, two natures (unmixed and unblended) in one Person, our friend listened with surprised interest, yet without understanding why or how God would do such a thing.

The previous chapters have explored the triune God and the human creature's relationship, by nature and grace, to the triune God. These chapters have made it possible for us to encounter far more profoundly Jesus Christ, who reveals the fullness of God and man to us.

The Promised Messiah

The Gospel of John tells us that when Andrew had met Jesus, he found his brother Simon Peter and said to him, "We have found the Messiah (which means Christ)" (Jn 1:41). The Messiah (in Hebrew) or the Christ (in Greek) signified the one who was anointed to redeem Israel. In the Old Covenant, the kings of Israel and Judah, as well as some of the prophets, were anointed by God. When David was being hunted by King Saul, at one point David had a chance to kill King Saul, but he refused to do so. David said, "I will not put forth my hand against my lord; for he is the Lord's anointed" (1 Sam 24:10). Psalm 2 expresses an intimate relation between the Lord and his anointed one: "The kings of the earth set themselves, and the rulers take counsel together, against the Lord and his anointed" (Ps 2:2). The Lord and his anointed are treated as one unit; the presence of the Lord's anointed indicates the presence of the Lord himself.

In light of the role of kings as the Lord's anointed ones in the Old Testament, another image takes on importance, that of shepherd. Psalm 23 depicts the Lord as the shepherd of Israel. The Davidic kings were also called "shepherds" of God's people. King David is said to have been an actual sheepherder before becoming shepherd, or king, over the United Kingdom of Israel. The kings, however, often did not shepherd in accord with the true interests of the sheep. The prophet Ezekiel denounces the kings of Israel: "Thus says the Lord God: Ho, shepherds of Israel who have been feeding yourselves! Should not shepherds feed the sheep?" (Ezek 34:2). This infidelity cuts at the heart of the covenant. The anointed kings were meant to be a sign of God's presence among men, but instead they became obstacles and even enemies of God. Ezekiel continues, "Thus says the Lord God, Behold, I am against the shepherds" (Ezek 34:10). God then promises, "I myself will be the shepherd of my sheep, and I will make them lie down, says the Lord God. I will seek the lost, and I will bring back the strayed" (Ezek 34:15–16).

It is in this context of the Old Testament that we must understand Jesus' words, "I am the good shepherd. The good shepherd lays down his life for the sheep" (Jn 10:11). Jesus simultaneously claims the role of the Old Testament kings and the role of the Lord who had promised one day to shepherd the people himself. The sinfulness of the Old Testament kings prevented them from acting in accord with God, rendering them unable to fulfill their role as the Lord's anointed. The Word of God solves this problem by taking on a human nature. As the Word of God, the Son of

God, he was intimately united with God the Father: "I and the Father are one" (Jn 10:30). As a human being, he could stand among human beings fulfilling the role of the Lord's anointed to mediate God's presence. Only God could shepherd us well; yet we could only *see* a human shepherd. Jesus Christ in his divine and human natures fulfills both needs. As the Book of Revelation says, "there were loud voices in heaven, saying, 'The kingdom of our world has become the kingdom of our Lord and of his Christ'" (Rev 11:15). Or as St. John and St. Paul put it: "The Word became flesh and dwelt among us, full of grace and truth" (Jn 1:14), and "In [Christ] the whole fullness of deity dwells bodily" (Col 2:9).

If the Incarnation of the Word accomplishes what was necessary, what happens after Jesus' Ascension when his human nature is no longer visibly present on earth? Christ does not leave his Church alone, but sends her the Paraclete, the Holy Spirit, to guide her. The Church, as the mystical Body of Christ, acts as the *ongoing incarnation* of our Lord Jesus Christ. This becomes more apparent when we return to the shepherd theme in the Gospel of John. Jesus does not stop after he claims to be the good shepherd. After his resurrection, Jesus establishes Simon Peter as the shepherd of his flock. Three times Jesus asks Peter, "Do you love me more than these?" Three times Peter says, "Yes, Lord." Three times, Jesus says to Peter, "Feed my sheep" (cf. Jn 21:15–17). Just as Jesus mediates the presence of the Father, so Peter, and the Petrine office as it develops, mediate the presence of Jesus. Teaching about his presence in and through the apostles and their successors, Jesus says, "Truly, truly, I say to you, he who receives any one whom I send receives me; and he who receives me receives him who sent me" (Jn 13:20).

Just before Jesus' death and resurrection, Philip asked Jesus, "Lord, show us the Father, and we shall be satisfied" (Jn 14:8). Jesus answered him, "Have I been with you so long, and yet you do not know me, Philip? He who has seen me has seen the Father" (Jn 14:9). It is crucial to recognize, before we proceed, that the speculative analysis involved in understanding the Incarnation—that is, the "hypostatic union" of the divine and human natures in the Person of the Son—is simply a way of articulating what is meant by Jesus' declaration that whoever has seen him has seen the Father.

God for Us

Why did God become incarnate? St. John describes it this way: "For God so loved the world that he gave his only Son, that whoever believes in him should not perish but have eternal life" (Jn 3:16). The force of this state-ment lies in the fact that it declares what the Incarnation accomplishes for us, namely, eternal life. Life eternal is simply another way of describing the ultimate end of man, or happiness. Life eternal describes the perfect union of the saints with God in heaven. How then does the Incarnation lead us to this goal?

The Incarnation leads us to eternal life in at least five ways. (3, q.1, a.2). First, it increases faith since faith is more certain now that it believes what God himself has spoken. Second, it increases the virtue of hope by showing the great mercy of God: "Be merciful, even as your Father is mer-ciful" (Lk 6:36). Third, the Incarnation enkindles charity since we know how deeply God loves us: "God shows his love for us in that while we were yet sinners Christ died for us" (Rom 5:8). Fourth, it encourages us to live rightly since God himself gives us the perfect example. As St. Augustine teaches, "Man who might be seen was not to be followed; but God was to be followed, Who could not be seen. And therefore God was made man, that he Who might be seen by man, and Whom man might follow, might be shown to man" (*Sermon* 22, *de Temp.*). Fifth, the Incarnation allows us to participate fully in divinity. Christ's humanity, our path to his divinity, accomplishes this. Again St. Augustine summarizes it eloquently: "God was made man, that man might be made God" (*Sermon* 13, *de Temp.*).

In order to move toward the good of human life, we need to move away from evil. This happens in several ways. First, the Incarnation heals the wound of our pride by showing us the humility of God. St. Paul writes, "Have this mind among yourselves, which was in Christ Jesus, who, though he was in the form of God, did not count equality with God a thing to be grasped, but emptied himself, taking the form of a servant, being born in the likeness of men" (Phil 2:5–7). Second, the Incarnation takes away our presumption that we can heal ourselves spiritually; God loves us in Christ Jesus even while we were still spiritually dead in our sins. Third, it shows the great dignity of human nature. If God has deigned to assume our nature, then we should avoid any evil deeds that would debase human nature. Finally, in order that the human race be freed from sin, Jesus Christ made satisfaction for our sins. God has not simply com-manded that the disorder caused by sin be repaired; he has come as a man to repair it from within human history.

In all of these ways, the Incarnation of the Word withdraws us from evil and sin and leads us to perfect happiness. We are set free from evil to move toward the good. Christ teaches us by enabling us to become *like* him in holiness. To do so, however, requires that we receive the forgiveness of sins. The Incarnation culminates in the cross, which reconciles sinners to God: "the New Law fulfills the Old by justifying men through the power of Christ's Passion" (1-2, q.107, a.2). There is a harmony or a beauty to the way God saves us through the Incarnation. God all-powerful could have saved us however he wished, but the Incarnation appears as the best and surest way to heal and transform the image of God within us. The movement toward good denotes our becoming like God; the withdrawal from evil signifies that God frees us from sin and the devil and even from debt owed to God. Redemption has two aspects: liberation from sin and union with God.

In short, the perfection of the Incarnation manifests itself in the way that it accomplishes both the negative and the positive elements of our salvation. We are turned from evil by repentance and the forgiveness of sins (Lk 24:47). We are led into eternal life by becoming children of God (Jn 1:12). These twin focal points—forgiveness of sins and divine filiation—form the center of the new life in Christ.

Christ as Example

Christ's centrality in our lives derives from the union of the divine and human natures in him. We can see him and follow him because he has assumed a human nature. Yet he is only *worthy* to be followed because he is the true God. St. Thomas notes that human beings must be led by the hand (*manuductio*) from sensible things to the knowledge of divine things. First among these sensible things is the humanity of Christ, which as an example stirs up our devotion. Because Christ is God, moreover, his teaching justifies us and makes us sharers in the divine life. The correspondence of teaching and example is important to grasp: Christ teaches us by giving us his example. This combination is evident from the Gospel of John: "You call me Teacher and Lord; and you are right, for so I am. If I, then, your Lord and Teacher, have washed your feet, you also ought to wash one another's feet. For I have given you an example, that you also should do as I have done to you" (Jn 13:13–15). Good teachers teach by the example of their lives. As St. Thomas says in his commentary on this passage from John, "examples move more than words" (*Commentary on John*, chap. 13, lecture 3; cf. 1-2, q.34, a.1).

What is included under the example of Christ? Are there different ways in which St. Thomas speaks of Christ as example? We can distinguish at least two levels of Christ's example: imitating Christ's actions (moral exemplarity) and imitating Christ's divine sonship by becoming children of God by grace (ontological exemplarity). Moral exemplarity is straightforward: Christ does good deeds, and we are supposed to imitate them. As we read in 1 John 2:6, "he who says he abides in [Jesus Christ] ought to walk in the same way in which he walked." Christians should imitate Christ's words, deeds, and ways of acting. St. Thomas recalls this moral exemplarity when he defends the teaching that there are several senses of Scripture. He writes, "in the New Law, whatever our Head has done is a type of what we ought to do" (1, q.1, a.10). For instance, if we ask why Christ experienced bodily defects, one of the reasons is that Christ gives us an example of patience by enduring bodily weariness and sufferings. The Christian therefore can look to Christ as an example of every virtue. He presents the pattern in word and deed; it is our task to imitate him. Imitation, however, includes much more than repetition of individual words and deeds. To imitate Christ is to follow along the way of Christ, that is, to follow along the way that is Christ himself.

Christ is not simply a good man who offers us an example, however. In Christ the *God* who became man offers us an example. God is the one who should be followed. Yet human beings have no way of imitating God, at least not according to their natural capacities. We are meant not merely to imitate the human nature of Christ, but to imitate the Person of Christ, the Word of God. Following Christ's divine example can be called *ontological exemplarity*. We can speak of this ontological exemplarity in terms of the example of sonship. This can be summarized as follows: We are called not only to imitate what Christ did, but to imitate who he is as the Son of God.

As St. Thomas shows, our *adoptive* filiation (or sonship) imitates Christ's *natural* filiation. As human beings adopt a child out of their goodness to share in their inheritance, so God in his infinite goodness admits creatures to share in his goodness. Above all, rational creatures are invited to share in God's goodness since they are made in the image of God and are thus capable of divine beatitude. God adopts human beings into the inheritance of his eternal beatitude. This is why divine adoption is greater than human adoption. Whereas human beings are already suitable to be adopted by other human beings, God makes us suitable for divine adoption, enabling us by the gift of grace to be "worthy to receive the heavenly inheritance" (3, q.23, a.1). The gift of our adoptive filiation flows out of God's infinite goodness, which desires to communicate itself to others. Christ as ontological example includes the form that his sonship took while on earth; adoptive filiation thus means sharing in the pattern of cross and resurrection. As Vatican II states, "Christ, the final Adam, by the revelation of the mystery of the Father and His love, fully reveals man to man himself" (*Gaudium et Spes* 22).

In discussing adoptive filiation, St. Thomas notes three ways that the Word of the Father can be imitated. First, creatures can imitate the Word according to their material form. On this level, all creatures imitate the Word since all things were made through the Word. Second, rational creatures can imitate the Word according to their intellectual form, as when they understand the world around them. In this second way, rational creatures (human beings and angels) imitate the Word of God by their rational being. Third, by grace and charity we imitate the Word of God according to the unity he has with the Father. This kind of likeness, which is divine filiation, can be had only by rational creatures who possess the virtue of charity. Only because human beings can be adopted children by grace can they hope to imitate all of the actions of the Son of God by nature: "By the grace of union Christ is the natural Son; whereas another man by habitual grace is an adopted son" (3, q.23, a.4, ad 2). The grace of the Holy Spirit is the grace of adoption.

The Mystery of Jesus Christ

Up to this point we have examined the way in which Christ saves us. Now we turn to the question of who Christ has to be in order to accomplish this. This order of proceeding is not accidental. We must guard against a distaste for the intricacies of Christological doctrines. In the centuries after Christ's death and resurrection, the Church never shied away from facing such doctrinal difficulties because she knew that if we misunderstand who Jesus is, then the reality of his salvation will be closed to us.

Following the creeds of the Church as formulated by the early Councils, St. Thomas holds that Jesus Christ possesses two natures, one human and one divine. Jesus Christ, however, only is one Person, the divine Person of the Son of God. The distinction between nature and person is recognized in everyday speech. If a child sees someone walking down the street and asks, "What is that?" the parent replies, "That's a man." If the child asks, "Who is that?" the parent says, "That's Uncle Charlie." The concept "nature" answers the question "What is it?" and the concept "person" answers the question "Who is it?" When the disciples saw Jesus and asked, "What is Jesus?" both answers would be correct, "That's a man" and "That's God." When the disciples asked, "Who is Jesus?" the answer would be "That's the Son of God, the Second Person of the Trinity." In fact, when Jesus asked, "Who do you say that I am?" Simon Peter answered, "You are the Christ, the Son of the living God" (Mt 16:15–16).

There have been many heresies about Jesus Christ that have sought to lessen what has been called "the scandal of the Incarnation." Some contend that it is unthinkable that God and man could be joined together in one person. And, in fact, it is true that the precise nature of that union is beyond our comprehension. Since the existence of God immeasurably surpasses creaturely existence, we cannot know the way in which the Son of God joined to himself a human nature. It remains a mystery—something above, not contrary to, human reason—how the Second Person of the Trinity was born of a virgin, lived, suffered, died, and rose again. This incomprehension, however, does not require that we turn off our intellects. The reverse is the case. *Because* the divine nature is beyond our comprehension, it can take to itself a human nature without ceasing to be divine.

Consider it this way. Try to imagine a dog-man who was fully canine and fully human. You cannot. The reason why the two natures are incompatible with each other is that they are both *created* natures. As created natures they occupy the same field of action. In this way, they are in a competitive relationship—either a dog or a man, but not both. Now consider the union of two natures, one divine and one human. Here there is a noncompetitive relationship because the divine nature is the source of the human nature, just as it is the source of every other created nature. Our inability to comprehend the divine nature stems from its distinction from creation.

Once this distinction between the Creator and his creation is recognized, then the Incarnation ceases to be a contradiction. It is a miracle, but not a logical impossibility. One being can be both God and man because the two natures do not exist side by side. Many of the early heresies about Christ viewed the divine and the human natures waging a turf-battle in the person of Jesus Christ. Many modern objectors to the Incarnation likewise assert that it is simply impossible for one thing to be both God and man. These objections err by treating the divine nature as simply another nature within the universe. Once God is confessed as the Creator, then the Incarnation can be confessed in a way that avoids contradiction.

It follows from the one person–two natures formula that there is, perhaps surprisingly, no human person in Jesus Christ. "Person" here means the subject to whom acts are attributed. His human nature is united to the divine nature at the instant of his conception, so he is never an autonomous subject or person. The subject to whom his acts are attributed is always the Person of the Word. Although there can be one person who acts through two natures, there cannot be two persons who act through two natures: this would divide the Incarnation, since the acts of the incarnate Son would no longer be attributed to one subject. If there were two persons, then our salvation would be jeopardized since the eternal Word of God would not have suffered for us on the cross (the heresy of Nestorius). The one Person in Christ is, of course, the eternal Word of God. Yet Christ is fully human because he possesses a full human nature—body and rational soul. Christ's humanity is elevated because it is brought into union with the Second Person of the Trinity. The Person of the Word continues to exist in his eternal divine nature and now exists as well in his human nature that he assumed in the womb of the Virgin Mary.

How does this assumption of a human nature take place? Without probing the mystery in a rationalistic way, St. Thomas helps us to avoid imagining the union of God with a human nature in a way that would jeopardize either Christ's full divinity or his full humanity. The human nature could not have been assumed *into* the divine nature, since this would result in an impossible conflation of divine and human. Christ is not a mix of divine and human elements (the heresy of Eutyches), but rather is both fully divine and fully human. If the union did not take place in the divine nature, then it must have taken place *in a divine Person*. Recall that a divine Person is not other than the divine nature, as if there were multiple gods. Rather, a divine Person is the divine nature as distinctly subsisting. The divine Persons are distinguished by relations of opposition, and thereby subsist in the nature distinctly. The union of the divine and the human natures could occur in the Person of the Word, therefore, because this would not imply that the divine nature had been altered, but would mean specifically that the Person of the Word now subsists in two ways, as God and as man. In subsisting as man, the Word does not lose his divinity: "the human nature assumed by the Word of God is ennobled, but the Word of God is not changed" (3, q.2, a.6, ad 1).

But is this really a "union"? If the divine nature and the human nature are still distinct as subsisting in the Person of the Word, can we truly call this a union? St. Thomas notes that the union of the two natures in the Word (traditionally called the hypostatic union, from the Greek word *hypostasis* for person) is in fact the greatest possible union. This is so because "the unity of the Divine Person, in which the two natures are united, is the greatest" (3, q.2, a.9). The unity of the divine Person is the unity of God. For the human nature to be united to the divine nature in the Word is to subsist in the Personal unity of the Word. Christ's divinity and humanity are utterly inseparable, though distinct.

This understanding of Jesus Christ allows us to speak correctly about him and to interpret correctly his deeds and words in the Gospels. It is true to say, as one of the early councils did, that "one of the Trinity suffered and died on the Cross." The Person of the Word is the only Person in Jesus Christ. The Person of the Word, therefore, is the only subject to whom we can attribute Christ's action. If someone asks how can God suffer since God is all-powerful and unchanging, then we can answer that the Word suffered not in his divine nature, but in his human nature. We also see in the Gospels Jesus performing great miracles over the physical forces of nature—the calming of the stormy sea and the raising of Lazarus. His human nature of itself had no power to perform these miracles. Yet his divine nature surely could do so. But the two natures cannot be separated since they are united in one person. In this way, whatever is done by the divine nature can be said of the human nature and vice versa.

This is called the communication of properties (*communicatio idiomata*). The suffering done by the human nature can be attributed to the divine nature. The miracles wrought by the divine nature can be attributed to the human nature. Since both natures are united in the one Person of Jesus Christ, we have God truly becoming a man without ceasing to be God. Christ's divinized human nature thus stands as the pattern after which we will also be divinized. Our divinization, however, is of a lesser order than Christ's since we become children of God not by nature, but by the adoption of grace. Nonetheless, the Incarnation of the Word makes possible the supernatural goal of human life, namely, sharing in God's own life.

The Humanity of Jesus Christ as the Instrument for the Full Revelation of God

Christ stands as the teacher of the new law of grace that alone can bring us to life with God. Only a teacher both divine and human could communicate this life to us. Through his humanity he communicates his divinity. But how is this possible? What are the conditions for Christ's humanity accomplishing this? First, Christ's humanity is conditioned by habitual grace. As subsisting in the Word, Christ's humanity has a unique relation to the Holy Spirit. The grace of the Holy Spirit conforms Christ's soul to the divine Word so that Christ's human knowing and loving might share in, and manifest, the divine life. As St. John writes, "the Word became flesh and dwelt among us, full of grace and truth" (Jn 1:14). Second, Christ possesses habitual grace not simply for himself, but also for us. In this way Christ is Head of his Mystical Body; he shares with us what we could never have obtained for ourselves. St. Thomas remarks that "grace was received by the soul of Christ in the highest way; and therefore from this pre-eminence of grace which he received, it is from him that this grace is bestowed on others,—and this belongs to the nature of head" (3, q.8, a.5). There is a communion between Christ and his members that truly makes us into "other Christs," as St. Cyril of Jerusalem put it.

Third, as we have already suggested, grace perfects Christ's human soul in such a way that his human intellect and will are fully conformed to his divinity. Christ, as the incarnate Son of God, has two intellects and two wills—divine and human. What Christ knows as God, he knows infinitely, eternally, and simply. Such knowledge is beyond the capacities of any finite intellect. In his humanity, however, Christ knows in a human way. His human mind is not dissolved into his divine mind, since the two operate on completely different levels. Nevertheless, grace elevates Christ's human knowing so that he can know and teach divine mysteries—in other words, so that his human intellect will truly be *conformed* uniquely to his divine intellect. Grace does not give Christ faith, as others receive. Christ teaches the divine mysteries in which believers have faith. If he had faith as we do, he would have no unique authority as a teacher. In addition, he teaches about himself in words that would be blasphemous did they not come from a supreme knowledge of his Father: "I and the Father are one" (Jn 10:30); "I have not spoken on my own authority; the Father who sent me has himself given me commandment what to say and what to speak" (Jn 12:49); "Let not your hearts be troubled; believe in God, believe also in me" (Jn 14:1).

St. Thomas therefore holds that along with acquired knowledge, Christ possessed the vision of God in his speculative intellect. He enjoyed the vision of God in perfect contemplative union, but the vision did not absorb all the powers of his intellect. He could still acquire knowledge in a fully human way. In fact, what Jesus knew in this contemplative vision could not, as a sharing in God's own nonconceptual knowledge, be expressed in finite concepts. To express what he knew by beatific vision in a manner accessible to the human mode of knowing, Christ needed both acquired knowledge and infused conceptual knowledge.

As the conformity of his human intellect with his divine intellect, Christ's vision of God enabled his words and deeds to express the divine Wisdom for all creatures. Just as St. Teresa of Avila's experience of moments of contemplative union shaped her words and deeds, so also, in a higher way, Christ's experiential knowledge of his Father in beatific vision illumined and governed his mission.

In similar fashion, grace conformed Christ's human will to his divine will. His supreme charity expresses God's will in sending his Son. His charity is grounded upon his knowledge, since what is not known cannot be loved. As Jesus says in the Gospel of John, "the Son can do nothing of his own accord, but only what he sees the Father doing; for whatever he does, that the Son does likewise. For the Father loves the Son, and shows him all that he himself is doing" (Jn 5:19–20). Christ's two wills act as one without negating his human free will. As we have seen, God can move the will by grace so that the will moves also on its own volition.

An important example of the conformity of human and divine in Christ is shown in his agony in the garden of Gethsemane, on the night before he was crucified. Sometimes Christ's agony is depicted as the breakdown of this conformity, but in fact the contrary is the case. Since the contemplative union of his human intellect with his divine intellect was unbroken, his ability to suffer intense sorrow—even agony—at Gethsemane was greatly intensified. In the garden of Gethsemane, Christ knew, far more than we ever could, what it means for humankind to reject his love. Likewise, his human will, while fully submitting to his divine will, fully experienced the natural human aversion to death.

As the divine Word, Christ in his humanity reveals the divine nature. He is the image of the invisible God. In knowing Christ, we come to know the Person of the Word of God. We know Christ through the human nature he has assumed, or, in the language of divine Personhood, through the human nature by which the Word now also subsists. When we come to know Christ, who is the Son and Word of God, the fullness of the God-head is revealed to us: the Son, through his Spirit, leads us to the Father. Jesus Christ reveals the Trinity of divine Persons. Although the human nature that Christ assumed cannot exhaust the mystery of God since it exists as a created nature, his human nature nevertheless remains the most fitting instrument for the revelation of God.

In this life, our knowledge of the Word remains imperfect, and hence we cannot be said to know *what God is*. But in the life to come, human knowledge of God will reach its perfection as the human intellect directly perceives the Word. It is worth emphasizing that Christ reveals God to us under the aspect of faith, not vision. The vision of God, including both intellectual and affective dimensions, can be had only in the beatific vision. As we have seen, Christ, who was both a wayfarer (*viator*) and one who comprehends (*comprehensor*), had the vision of God in his earthly life. We, however, who are merely wayfarers, live by faith. In the words of Saint Paul, "now we see in a mirror dimly, but then face to face" (1 Cor 13:12). Yet the answer to the question—what does Christ teach?—proves to be "God himself."

In short, Christ unleashes a new power for supernatural life into the world: "I came that they may have life, and have it abundantly" (Jn 10:10). He communicates this divine life into the world because he is the full revelation of God. When God the Father reveals himself through God the Son, he not merely reveals facts about himself. He communicates himself. The good news of the Incarnation contains explicit doctrines and practices because we are embodied, rational creatures who can only comprehend things through intellectual concepts and physical reality. Through these explicit doctrines and practices, however, God *gives himself* to his people. As St. Paul quotes the Old Testament, "I will be their God, and they shall be my people" (2 Cor 6:16). Why, then, is the Incarnation good news? Through the Incarnation, God reveals his mercy toward sinners and his desire to bring us back to himself. This divine mercy is the meaning of Christ's passion, death, and resurrection; everything discussed in this chapter depends upon the cross. It is to this that we now turn.

CHAPTER SIX

SALVATION

A college friend returned from post-graduation trips to Turkey and India. Not being a Christian, she remarked to her family that after seeing so many depictions of the crucified Christ in the ancient Christian basilicas of Turkey, she was relieved to get to India, where there were such positive images of the divine—sleek, voluptuous statues of male and female gods and goddesses, rather than a man hanging from a cross.

From the moment of his baptism by John and the inauguration of his public ministry, Jesus knowingly and willingly journeyed toward his crucifixion. As Jesus tells Pilate, "For this I was born, and for this I have come into the world, to bear witness to the truth" (Jn 18:37). Nonetheless, all of us have sometimes wondered why God chose a cross—the bloody death of his incarnate Son—to bring about the salvation of the world. Why did God humble himself so radically, in Jesus Christ, as to die a criminal in the most humiliating form of death?

When the risen Jesus explains why his cross is the light of salvation, rather than an absurd death, he reminds his followers to search the Old Testament which prepared for him: "Then he said to them, 'O foolish men, and slow of heart to believe all that the prophets have spoken! Was it not necessary that the Christ should suffer these things and enter into his glory?' And beginning with Moses and all the prophets, he interpreted to them in all the scriptures the things concerning himself" (Lk 24:25–27). Imitating Christ, St. Thomas allows his theology of salvation to be formulated in the context of biblical Israel's Mosaic Law and Temple, both of which are fulfilled by Christ and his Mystical Body.

Christ's Fulfillment of the Mosaic Law

It is impossible to understand why God chose the cross as the means of our salvation unless we first have a keen sense of what it means to be burdened by our own injustice and to live in a world marked by injustice. When we recognize the horror of injustice in the world, we are prepared to understand what Christ was teaching and doing for us. The first human beings lost their relationship with God by an act of contempt for their creator. As St. Augustine put it, the result was that "two cities were created by two kinds of love: the earthly city was created by self-love reaching the point of contempt for God, the Heavenly City by the love of God carried as far as contempt of self" (*City of God*, book 14, chap. 28).

Since the first human beings fell through disobedience, and this disobedience—with its violence, greed, envy, lust, and domination—has marked human history ever since, Christ's salvific action must be an act of supreme self-giving obedience. St. Thomas recognizes that Christ's supreme act of obedience—his cross or "passion"—fulfills the Mosaic Law given by God on Mt. Sinai (3, q.47, a.2, ad 1). In the Gospel of Matthew, Jesus teaches, "Think not that I have come to abolish the law and the prophets; I have come not to abolish them but to fulfil them. For truly, I say to you, till heaven and earth pass away, not an iota, not a dot, will pass from the law until all is accomplished" (5:17–18). In the Gospel of John, his final words from the cross are "It is finished" (19:30). He can be understood to mean that the Mosaic Law has been consummated or fulfilled in him, thereby inaugurating the new law of grace. In St. Paul's words, "as one man's trespass led to condemnation for all men, so one man's act of righteousness leads to acquittal and life for all men" (Rom 5:18).

Why would Jesus' cross be able to accomplish so great a thing as to fulfill all justice and restore the relationship with God that was lost by sin? Why would death on a cross, even the death of the incarnate Son of God, bring this about?

St. Thomas's answer relies upon his earlier analysis of the Mosaic Law, which we discussed above. He states that Jesus' cross simultaneously fulfills the three aspects of the Mosaic Law: its moral, ceremonial, and judicial precepts or laws. We can therefore examine the cross from three different perspectives, each of which illumines how it accomplishes our salvation. First, Jesus' perfect charity on the cross perfectly fulfilled the moral precepts of the Law, as embodied by the Ten Commandments. As Jesus says in the Gospel of John, "Greater love has no man than this, that a man lay down his life for his friends" (Jn 15:13).

Second, in the self-sacrifice that he offered upon the cross, Jesus perfectly fulfilled the ceremonial precepts, which prescribed the manner in which the Israelites were to render just worship to God. The author of the Epistle to the Hebrews put it this way: "every priest [of the Temple] stands daily at his service, offering repeatedly the same sacrifices, which can never take away sins. But when Christ had offered for all time a single sacrifice for sins, he sat down at the right hand of God" (Heb 10:11–12).

Third, when Christ, though innocent, took upon himself the suffering due to all others, he perfectly fulfilled the judicial precepts. As Isaiah prophesied, comparing the Messiah to a sin offering (such as would have been offered at Israel's Temple), "Surely he has borne our griefs and carried our sorrows; yet we esteemed him stricken, smitten by God, and afflicted. But he was wounded for our transgressions, he was bruised for our iniquities; upon him was the chastisement that made us whole, and with his stripes we are healed. All we like sheep have gone astray; we have turned every one to his own way; and the Lord has laid on him the iniquity of us all" (Isa 53:4–6).

Since the divine law is one, this fulfillment is *not a revocation*. In Christ, as we will see, believers participate in his fulfillment of the Mosaic Law. Meditating upon the three kinds of precepts in the old law draws us into the mystery of the new. Employing traditional terms for describing what Christ has accomplished for us—such as redemption, satisfaction, merit, and sacrifice—St. Thomas gains a deeper understanding of what the Mosaic Law prefigured and how Jesus saved humankind.

The Ceremonial Precepts: Christ as Priest

It is helpful to begin with the ceremonial precepts since they stand at the heart of the meaning of the cross. As we have seen, the ceremonial precepts of the Mosaic Law were primarily those precepts instituting the sacrificial system for worship. In contrast to the modern view of sacrificial offerings, St. Thomas attributes to sacrifice a *positive* symbolic force. Christ's sacrifice is prefigured in the Mosaic Law by three kinds of sacrifices: burnt offerings, peace offerings, and sin offerings. Christ's sacrifice is total (as prefigured by burnt offerings) and is, as an act of love, an act of praise and thanksgiving (as prefigured by peace offerings). As a sin offering, Christ's sacrifice operates—accomplishes its purpose—according to the modes of redemption and satisfaction. The concepts of redemption and satisfaction help us understand the numerous New Testament passages, such as 1 John 2:2, Ephesians 5:2, 1 Peter 1:18, Galatians 3:13, John 8:36, Revelation 1:5, and Romans 3:25, that attribute to Christ's cross an effect that restores humankind to its intended position vis-à-vis God.

To grasp the meaning of redemption requires an understanding of sin as a violation of the order of justice. To be in relation to God, who is perfect love, human beings must love. As we have seen, when the first human beings broke off this relationship by an act of contempt, the order of justice and love that united humankind to God was broken. With the exception of Jesus and the Virgin Mary (whom we will discuss later), all human beings since the Fall have been marked by this brokenness. This brokenness is a debt or wound in our relationship with God. The debt is "mortal" or deadly: eternal punishment consists in bearing this wound forever, knowing that, as children of Adam, we freely chose to separate ourselves from the one who alone can make us happy.

Clearly, if we could just turn around and love God perfectly again, we would be restored. The problem is that our wound or debt lies in our wills, which are disordered. Our choices lead us away from God, not toward him. As a sinless man, however, Christ did not owe the debt. Since Christ is God and man, the debt is more than redeemed by his sacrifice of his bodily life, as the life of the Son of God. Christ's cross accomplishes redemption because he shows perfect love in freely bearing the deadly punishment that sinners deserve. He redeems or pays the debt by restoring the order of justice between humankind and God. The order of justice is revealed as an order of God's gracious love.

Put another way, Christ makes satisfaction for what was lost by humankind's sins. St. Anselm developed the concept of satisfaction that St. Thomas uses: "He properly satisfies for an offense who offers something which the offended one loves equally, or even more than he detested the offense." The just penalty (or result) of the interior disorder caused by original sin is sensible pain and suffering, culminating in death: "For the wages of sin is death, but the free gift of God is eternal life in Christ Jesus our Lord" (Rom 6:23). In order to restore souls to justice, a human being would need freely to undergo suffering and death as the just penalty of sin, so that the disorder might be healed interiorly by obedience (the opposite of the sinful disobedience). By freely embracing the penalty as it embodies God's order of justice, Christ satisfied for all sins. His act accomplishes the salvation of all because of the unity of humankind before God that results not only from membership in the same species, but also from Christ's all-embracing charity.

Christ's sacrifice restores intrinsically the just relationship between all of humankind and God. Yet this universal reconciliation has to be appropriated by each of us through membership in Christ's Mystical Body by faith and charity. St. Paul opens our eyes to the deepest meaning of Christ's satisfaction: "Therefore, if anyone is in Christ, he is a new creation; the old has passed away, behold, the new has come. All this is from God, who through Christ reconciled us to himself and gave us the ministry of reconciliation; that is, God was in Christ reconciling the world to himself, not counting their trespasses against them, and entrusting to us the message of reconciliation. . . . We beseech you on behalf of Christ, be reconciled to God. For our sake he made him to be sin who knew no sin, so that in him we might become the righteousness of God" (2 Cor 5:17–21). Reconciliation is the heart of the good news.

The Moral Precepts: Christ as Prophet

Like the prophets of the Old Testament, who recognized love as the primary element of sacrifice and indeed of worship, St. Thomas does not separate Christ's cross from Christ's love. Christ's charity is what enables his cross to reconcile us to God and to each other. By teaching the new law of grace on the cross, Christ shows himself to be the true prophet. Even though the moral precepts of the Mosaic Law concern natural rather than supernatural virtues, it is impossible completely to fulfill the Mosaic Law without the supernatural virtue of charity. St. Thomas states, "Man cannot fulfil all the precepts of the law, unless he fulfil the precept of charity" (1-2, q.100, a.10, ad 3). Although the Ten Commandments do not include the command to love God, this law is found in Deuteronomy: "You shall therefore love the Lord your God, and keep his charge, his statutes, his ordinances, and his commandments always" (Deut 11:1). By his cross, Christ perfectly teaches this charity and enables us to share in it.

Why was Christ's charity so beneficial? The answer lies in his relationship with his heavenly Father. Although it might seem that charity is the same in every person who possesses charity, in fact there are various degrees of charity, corresponding to the degree of the person's participation in the Holy Spirit. To love God fully, one must know God fully. On earth, only Christ, because of his enjoyment of the vision of God, displayed this most perfect charity. Even the Virgin Mary, whose mind was not united to God by vision but only by faith, did not approach the degree of charity possessed by Christ.

As the fruit of his grace, therefore, Christ's charity merits a reward. Christ's sacrificial love is rewarded by the resurrection and glorification of his body. This reward is nothing else than God crowning his own gifts, since it gives glory to the divine justice. However, the merits of Christ's cross also bring about our salvation. In suffering for justice's sake out of supernatural charity, Christ merits not only for himself, but also for his members. His habitual grace is the same as his grace of Headship: the Holy Spirit perfects his human soul not only for him, but for us. Christ is the source of a mystical communion in which his resources overflow into all who are united to him by faith. St. Thomas notes that the result is that Christ's Mystical Body forms, as it were, one individual: "Christ's works are referred to Himself and to His members in the same way as the works of any other man in a state of grace are referred to himself" (3, q.48, a.1). When, full of grace, he merits by his sacrificial charity—his complete gift of self—the resurrection and glorification of his body, he merits the same for all his members.

The Judicial Precepts: Christ as King

How do the Mosaic Law's judicial precepts teach us about Christ's cross? On first glance, the ceremonial and moral precepts might seem more fitted to illumining salvation. When asked to offer an explanation for the mystery of the crucifixion, it helps to view it in light of the laws for behavior and sacrificial worship that we find in the Mosaic Law, since this pattern helps make sense of why God chooses to reconcile human beings through Christ's cross. But how do the judicial precepts, having to do with punishment, familial relations, and exchange, shed light on Christ's action?

The judicial precepts prefigured Christ's work, but not in the same way that the ceremonial precepts did. By shaping the government of Israel, they suggested the right order that should exist between human beings, but in practice, like any human politics, they were unable to produce this right order. Although God could have restored this right order simply by command, God chose to restore the order of justice not by command, but by Christ's supreme act of self-giving. He imposes nothing arbitrarily; rather he heals us from within.

The task of the king in Israel was to establish justice among his people. Christ, the true king, establishes justice for all humankind by his suffering, as the one who bears or endures their suffering due for sin. Christ fulfilled the judicial precepts by undergoing the greatest suffering. Only the incarnate Son who, filled with the Holy Spirit, knows fully the divine glory—the infinite wisdom and love of the Father, who loves us infinitely—could know fully what it means to oppose and reject this love. Therefore the depth of Christ's sorrow, in suffering for our sins, is beyond anything we could imagine. Moreover, in contrast to the limited scope of the actions of a mere man, Christ's suffering fulfills the judicial precepts because he could direct his intense suffering to the case of each human being. While suffering our penalty, he willed that his suffering serve the end of our being united with God. He freely suffered for our sins, and the Father freely gave him over to suffering, so that we might be blessed.

As St. Paul teaches, "Christ redeemed us from the curse of the law, having become a curse for us—for it is written, 'Cursed be every one who hangs on a tree'—that in Christ Jesus the blessing of Abraham might come upon the Gentiles, that we might receive the promise of the Spirit through faith" (Gal 3:13–14). Because Christ has suffered for us, our suffering is not meaningless, but actually draws us closer to Christ in charity. Carrying our own crosses, we are united with the God who has gone to the length of suffering for and with us, and share in his fulfillment of the Mosaic Law. "Now I rejoice in my sufferings for your sake, and in my flesh I complete what is lacking in Christ's afflictions for the sake of his body, that is, the church" (Col 1:24).

By recognizing that Christ's cross fulfills the three kinds of precepts of the Mosaic Law, St. Thomas develops a theology of salvation that profoundly balances Christ's sacrifice, Christ's charity, and Christ's suffering for others. He also shows why God gave such a prominent place in ancient Israel to the roles of priest, prophet, and king. In fulfilling the ceremonial precepts, Jesus is supremely priest; in fulfilling the moral precepts, he is supremely prophet or lawgiver (giving the law of love); and in fulfilling the judicial precepts, he is supremely king, losing his own life to establish justice among his people. Sometimes we hear it said that Christ's suffering and death were random violence. In God's plan, far from being random, they were the fulfillment of all justice—the righteousness of God—that the people of the Old Testament had been awaiting.

Christ's Fulfillment of Israel's Temple

St. Thomas's understanding of salvation does not stop with the cross. It is necessary to grasp the power of the cross, but we would never understand salvation from this alone. After all, Christ rises from the dead and ascends to heavenly glory! The other mysteries of Christ's life take their bearings from the cross, but they also cause our salvation in their own ways.

We can illumine this relationship by once again turning to the Old Testament. Christ's cross fulfills all justice, and thereby fulfills the Mosaic Law and reconciles everything on earth and in Heaven (cf. Col 1:20). The other mysteries of Christ's life—preeminently his Incarnation, transfiguration, resurrection, and ascension—indicate the ways that we are united with the life of the Trinity. These mysteries reveal how human beings become temples of the triune God. They reveal how Christ's perfect worship on the cross fulfills Israel's *Temple*.

1 Kings 8 is the key biblical passage for understanding Israel's Temple. The chapter describes the dedication of the new Temple by King Solomon, who in a dedicatory speech sets forth the spiritual significance of the Temple. In this speech, Solomon asks,

> But will God indeed dwell on the earth? Behold, heaven and the highest heaven cannot contain thee; how much less this house which I have built! Yet have regard to the prayer of thy servant and to his supplication, O Lord my God, hearkening to the cry and to the prayer which thy servant prays before thee this day; that thy eyes may be open night and day toward this house, the place of which thou hast said, 'My name shall be there,' that thou mayest hearken

to the prayer which thy servant offers toward this place. And hearken thou to the supplication of thy servant and thy people Israel, when they pray toward this place; yea, hear thou in heaven thy dwelling place; and when thou hearest, forgive. (1 Kings 8:27–30)

This passage contains two key elements: first, God infinitely transcends the Temple (8:27); and second, God has nonetheless chosen to place his "name" there (8:29).

In St. Thomas's view, the promise that God's "name" would dwell in the Temple meant that the liturgy of the Temple, that is, the prayers of the people who participate in the Temple worship, would express God's true identity. The Book of Revelation takes up this theme as characteristic of the true Temple: "He who conquers, I will make him a pillar in the temple of my God; never shall he go out of it, and I will write on him the name of my God, and the name of the city of my God, the new Jerusalem which comes down from my God out of heaven, and my own new name" (Rev 3:12). We are made into the true Temple, the Mystical Body of Christ, by sharing in God's "name" or identity—by our graced sharing in "He who is," the divine life of blessedness. Thus, the emphasis in the Old Testament on the Temple as the place of true worship is connected by the New Testament with Christ's perfect worship (on the cross) and human beings' participation in Christ's perfect worship as members of his Mystical Body.

Once we realize that believers are a "temple" of the Holy Spirit, we can never think about life the same way again. "Do you not know," asks St. Paul, "that you are God's temple and that God's Spirit dwells in you?" (1 Cor 3:16). This is the salvation that God, in Christ, is offering us—to rejoice inexhaustibly in the mysteries of God's love and wisdom.

The Incarnation: Manifested in Mary

We discussed the Incarnation in the previous chapter. In this chapter we will focus upon a new element, St. Thomas's teachings about the Virgin Mary. Her role in the Incarnation is significant. She is intensely active in the life of her Son, rather than a mere impersonal "receptacle" through which Jesus passes. Just as God promised that his "name" would dwell in the Temple, the Virgin Mary receives the promise that the child that she will conceive by the power of the Holy Spirit "will be called holy, the Son of God" (Lk 1:35).

Recognizing this parallel, St. Thomas teaches that the full meaning of God's "presence" in the Temple and of the Temple's holiness is powerfully revealed in the Virgin Mary's relation to God. In his view, Psalm 46:4 (as it reads in the ancient Greek translation called the "Septuagint"), "The most High has sanctified his tabernacle," prefigures the Virgin Mary's sanctification by the Holy Spirit. St. Thomas knows that the Bible, in its literal sense, does not teach Mary's perfect holiness directly: "Nothing is handed down in the canonical Scriptures concerning the sanctification of the Blessed Mary as to her being sanctified in the womb; indeed, they do not even mention her birth" (3, q.27, a.1). He points out that the same is true about Mary's assumption to Heaven, which is nonetheless testified to by the Fathers. He therefore turns largely to the Old Testament to show that Mary, in order to play her role in the Incarnation, must have been specially sanctified.

In light of the frequent images of the Temple's holiness in the Old Testament, St. Thomas reasons that God must have made the "temple" that housed his incarnate Son worthy of receiving God incarnate. God's name can abide only in a place that is characterized by holy actions. The Virgin Mary, as the temple that received God's incarnate presence, therefore must have been holy. She becomes the conduit of God's Word because of her great holiness, which is a gift of God. Furthermore, in her "Yes"—her *fiat*—to God at the Annunciation, she answers not only for herself but for the whole created order that will be redeemed by Christ. She must be able to give herself totally, without reserve. After all, the Annunciation does not simply inform Mary of what was to come, but also initiates, in St. Thomas's words, "a certain spiritual wedlock between the Son of God and human nature" (3, q.30, a.1). As an event analogous to marriage—the marriage of God and human nature—the Incarnation required the consent of the betrothed, and so "the Virgin's consent was besought in lieu of that of the entire human nature" (ibid.). St. Thomas highlights Mary's role in the Incarnation in order to show that the Incarnation is not simply a preparation for the cross, but the inauguration of the fulfilled Temple, the visible Mystical Body of Christ.

Certain problems are raised by St. Thomas's interpretation. First, his view of *when* Mary's sanctification occurred differs from the doctrine of the Immaculate Conception of Mary. In 1854 the Catholic Church formally taught that Mary was preserved from sin, by the grace of Christ, from the very moment of her conception. St. Thomas teaches that Mary was not sanctified at the instant of her conception, but was sanctified before her birth from the womb. Still, the general affinity of St. Thomas's teaching with the doctrine is much greater than its point of disagreement.

Second, people may wonder how, if Mary was sanctified and committed no sins, she still had free will (the same question that is raised against Jesus' sinlessness). We are actually *more* free the less we are held in bondage to sin. As St. Paul, speaking of the pitiful condition of sinners, remarks, "I delight in the law of God, in my inmost self, but I see in my members another law at war with the law of my mind and making me captive to the law of sin which dwells in my members. Wretched man that I am! Who will deliver me from this body of death? Thanks be to God through Jesus Christ our Lord!" (Rom 7:22–25). The less we are inclined to sin, the more free our wills truly are.

Third, Mary was made holy before Christ's cross. Her sanctification, however, comes through Christ's merits, since the grace of the Holy Spirit always comes to us through Christ. As St. Thomas writes, "The Blessed Virgin was sanctified in the womb from original sin, as to the personal stain; but she was not freed from the guilt to which the whole nature is subject, so as to enter into Paradise otherwise than through the Sacrifice of Christ" (3, q.27, a.1, ad 3). In her holiness, she is evidence that people before Christ were not cut off from the salvation won by Christ. This also is an important element for our understanding of salvation. We will discuss this point further in discussing the Church. The crucial aspect is that her role in the Incarnation manifests the Mystical Body, the fulfillment of Israel's Temple.

The Transfiguration

Jesus Christ himself is the most perfect fulfillment of Israel's Temple. He is the ultimate source for understanding God's indwelling in us, since he mediates this indwelling to all other human beings. The transfiguration begins to reveal how human beings, united to Christ, will share eternally in the divine life. St. Matthew's Gospel tells us that "after six days Jesus took with him Peter and James and John his brother, and led them up a high mountain apart. And he was transfigured before them, and his face shone like the sun, and his garments became white as light. And behold, there appeared to them Moses and Elijah, talking with him" (Mt 17:1–3). In light of Genesis, the "after six days" is significant: the seventh day symbolizes the completion of creation, which is now about to occur in the fulfilled Temple.

If suffering (dying on a cross) were all that we knew of Christ, who would follow him? The transfiguration thus prepares us for his resurrection and ascension. In Christ's transfigured body, we see that God will transform us into persons who can rejoice spiritually and bodily in eternal life. The transfiguration shows members of Christ's Mystical Body that their suffering leads to glory. St. Thomas teaches, "Our Lord, after foretelling His Passion to His disciples, had exhorted them to follow the path of His sufferings (Mt 16:21, 24). Now in order that anyone go straight along a road, he must have some knowledge of the end. . . . Above all is this necessary when hard and rough is the road, heavy the going, but delightful the end" (3, q.45, a.1). The transfiguration is about the "end"— the fulfilled Temple, the perfect presence of God.

Why did Christ choose "shining" (clarity) to manifest, in his body, the glory of the fulfilled Temple? Clarity is the spiritual glory (holiness) of the soul overflowing into the body. This miracle occurred when Christ's face "shone like the sun." We have all seen people who seem to glow with happiness or with love. The outward glow indicates an inward peace. Clarity then was a way to manifest the "end" of the fulfilled Temple, in which all will be united by perfect holiness and love. St. Thomas emphasizes this application to the Mystical Body by distinguishing between the resplendence of Christ's face and his garments. He writes, "Just as the clarity which was in Christ's body was a representation of His body's future clarity, so the clarity which was in His garments signified the future clarity of the saints, which will be surpassed by that of Christ, just as the brightness of the snow is surpassed by that of the sun" (3, q.45, a.2, ad 3). Christ's whole Mystical Body will shine, but the source of its shining will always be Christ himself.

The transfiguration reveals the coming fulfillment of Israel's Temple in two other ways. First, Moses and Elijah, along with the three chief disciples, were chosen to appear with Christ. This reveals the unity of the divine law; salvation includes not only those after Christ, but also those before him, and for both Christ is the source of salvation. As St. Thomas notes, "men are brought to the glory of eternal beatitude by Christ,—not only those who lived after Him, but also those who preceded Him" (3, q.45, a.3).

Second, at the transfiguration, God the Father, speaking out of the "cloud" (symbolic of the Holy Spirit), says, "This is my beloved Son, with whom I am well pleased; listen to him" (Mt 17:5). A similar manifestation of the Trinity had occurred at Christ's baptism. Baptism takes away sin and confers innocence; the transfiguration prefigures the "end" or goal of baptism, namely, the conferring of heavenly glory in the fulfilled Temple. The event of the transfiguration reveals that Christ is about to bring Israel's Temple to its fulfillment in his Mystical Body.

The Resurrection and Ascension

In the Gospel of Matthew, the witnesses against Jesus say, "This fellow said, 'I am able to destroy the temple of God, and to build it in three days'" (Mt 26:61). The Gospel of John confirms this in its account of Jesus' cleansing of the Temple: "Jesus answered them, 'Destroy this temple, and in three days I will raise it up. . . . But he spoke of the temple of his body. When therefore he was raised from the dead, his disciples remembered that he had said this; and they believed the scripture and the word which Jesus had spoken" (Jn 2:19–22).

Both Gospels suggest that the disciples recognized only after his resurrection why Jesus had to suffer. The disciples had tried to prevent him from allowing himself to be crucified. Now they understand that the purpose of Jesus' sacrificial charity on the cross was none other than to establish the heavenly (fulfilled) Temple. In fact, as they now recognize, Jesus himself *is* this Temple. By sharing in his self-giving love, human beings are united to him and become pillars of the true Temple.

In distinguishing between the causality of Christ's cross and of his resurrection as regards our salvation, St. Thomas notes that "Christ's Passion wrought our salvation, properly speaking, by removing evils; but the Resurrection did so as the beginning and exemplar of all good things" (3, q.53, a.1, ad 3; cf. Rom 4:25). This is the distinction between efficient and exemplar causality that we saw earlier. The cross restores justice and fulfills the Mosaic Law; the resurrection manifests human glorification and fulfills Israel's Temple. Christ's resurrection is the exemplar cause of the future resurrection of all human beings. Had Christ not been resurrected, we would never have had the hope that our bodies would truly share in eternal glory. If Christ's resurrection is good news for all human beings, however, why did he not show himself to everyone after his resurrection? Christ showed himself only to a few, who then spread the good news, because evangelization is the task of the Mystical Body on earth.

After his resurrection Christ did not stay on earth, but ascended to his Father in heaven. St. Thomas holds that the ascension is the means by which Christ "prepared the way for our ascent into heaven. . . . For since He is our Head the members must follow whither the Head has gone" (3, q.57, a.6). Indeed, when he ascended to heaven, the souls of the holy men and women who had been waiting in the "hell of the just" for his cross to take away the debt of original sin, ascended with him. Ever since Christ's resurrection and ascension, the Mystical Body, Israel's fulfilled Temple, has been present in heaven. Now that Christ is in heaven with his saints, he intercedes for those who are still journeying toward him. Citing Ephesians 4:10, St. Thomas notes that Christ ascended so that "being established in His heavenly seat as God and Lord, He might send down gifts upon men" (3, q.57, a.6). These gifts are the subject of the next chapter.

CHAPTER SEVEN

CHURCH AND SACRAMENTS

The Church's worship is full of references to the whole of human history. The liturgy reminds us of the blessings of creation, God's covenants with Israel, the saving work of Jesus Christ, and the saints and angels, who, together with those present at the liturgy, offer the prayers of the whole Church to God. The stained glass windows in the great cathedrals made graphic this wondrous communion, spanning all of human history. The gargoyles warned that evil must be fought by all generations. Although Christ has won the victory, we must be united with Christ through our own sufferings and the struggle against sin in our lives. The pattern of the Church's worship makes clear that as the true teacher, Christ instructs us through his Church and her sacraments. As grade school teachers instruct by means of words and visual aids accessible to their students, Christ imparts to us the gift of the Holy Spirit through words and signs accessible to our present state. This insight guides our presentation of the Church and her sacraments.

The History of Salvation

The nature of the Church cannot be understood without first grasping its role in human history. We cannot focus here upon the history of the Church through the past two thousand years.

That would cause us to miss the forest for the trees. Instead, understanding the Church's role in human history requires a "theology of history" in which history itself is illumined by faith. St. Thomas identifies four "states" in humankind's return to God: the state before the Law, the state of the Old Law, the state of the New Law, and the state of glory—that is, heaven. The first three states are ordered to the fourth, and are intended to prepare human beings for the perfect worship of God. By means of these four states, St. Thomas shows how time and place are related to the reality of the Church. Although the Church only is fully manifested after Christ, it is present in all ages. Let us see what this means.

After the coming of Jesus Christ, the Mystical Body is always visible as the Catholic Church. The Catholic Church truly is Christ's Mystical Body. Yet, because the Church is a "mystical" or spiritual reality, its reality goes beyond what is visible. Persons who do not belong to the visible Church may well belong to the Mystical Body, and persons who by all appearances belong to the visible Church may not actually be members of the Mystical Body. In fact, the Mystical Body is composed of all those who have been gathered by the Holy Spirit into a communion of charity with Christ. Throughout history, the Holy Spirit has been active invisibly drawing people to Christ's love. In all times and places, there have been people who have believed, at least implicitly, in Christ, and have been sharers in Christ's new law, which is the grace of the Holy Spirit. As the famous "hall of faith" in Hebrews 11 suggests, there have been people, from Abel to Moses, who were pleasing to God by faith before Christ. Faith in Christ does not necessarily require *explicit* knowledge of him. Following the insights of Hebrews 11, St. Thomas's understanding of implicit faith in Christ includes, in places where the biblical revelation is unknown, those people who believed "in Divine providence, since they believed that God would deliver mankind in whatever way was pleasing to Him" (2-2, q.2, a.7, ad 3). The author of Hebrews writes that "without faith it is impossible to please [God]. For whoever would draw near to God must believe that he exists and that he rewards those who seek him" (Heb 11:6). Just as the Gospel teaches that "there is nothing hid, except to be made manifest" (Mk 4:22), God will bring people from implicit faith to the explicit confession that "Jesus is Lord" (1 Cor 12:3).

The outpouring of the grace of the Holy Spirit at Pentecost, however, is explosive: now that Christ has come, the Holy Spirit acts upon the world in extraordinary ways. Hearing the good news gives human beings, at long last, direct evidence for hope that sin, suffering, and death will truly be conquered by love. As Jesus tells his disciples in the Gospel of Matthew, "Truly, I say to you, many prophets and righteous men longed to see what you see, and did not see it, and to hear what you hear, and did not hear it" (Mt 13:17). When we realize that Jesus truly has saved us from the condition of separation from God in which we were mired by our own injustice, then we understand how blessed we are to know Jesus. Thus, the *fullness* of the Church is manifested only after Christ's cross and resurrection. Christ's Body becomes present in the world as a communion of people united by hearing Christ's word and by partaking in his sacramental presence. As a visible communion with a visible presence in history, the Church is led by the apostles and their successors the bishops, led by the bishop of Rome as the successor of St. Peter.

God gives grace to all people, not just those who have been privileged to hear the good news of salvation. Why then bother spreading the good news by inviting others to share in the Church's teachings and sacraments? St. Thomas explains that the condition of human beings, both in their relationship to God and in their relationships with one another, has been radically changed by God's actions in history. Throughout all of human history, some people are joined to Christ by faith and charity, but the dual events of the giving of the Mosaic Law and the explicit proclamation of the New Law of grace radically transformed humankind. The good news is now publicly announced throughout the world and the sacraments are administered. Through the Church and her sacraments, God now imparts grace to us in the manner best suited to our nature as creatures with body and soul. We see these blessings most vividly in the saints, but also in the small acts of faith, hope, and love that are often hidden and always a cause for rejoicing.

The Nature of the Church

St. Thomas describes Christ as "our wisest and greatest friend" (1-2, q.108, a.4). Since Christ's Person is divine, friendship with the man Christ entails intimate friendship with God. The Church is the community constituted by this friendship. St. Thomas did not, therefore, write a separate treatise on "the Church." Rather, in writing about friendship with

Christ, he shows how Christ makes his Church—his community of friends—united and filled with his grace. As we put it in the previous chapter, by becoming friends with Christ through participation in his sacrifice on the cross, we become members of the fulfilled Temple, the Mystical Body of Christ. Christ on the cross teaches the new law and thus, by the grace of the Holy Spirit, leads us to the Father as members of his Mystical Body. The new law is primarily Christ's gift of the Holy Spirit who dwells in the faithful, and so his Mystical Body cannot be understood without grasping the formative role of the Holy Spirit and the sacraments of the new law.

As St. Paul says, Christ "is the head of the body, the church; he is the beginning, the first-born from the dead, that in everything he might be pre-eminent. For in him all the fulness of God was pleased to dwell, and through him to reconcile to himself all things, whether on earth or in heaven, making peace by the blood of his cross" (Col 1:18–20). The Holy Spirit is the divine Person who, in the Mystical Body, knits together Head and members. St. Thomas suggests that "the Holy Spirit is likened to the heart, since He invisibly quickens and unifies the Church" (3, q.8, a.1, ad 3). The Holy Spirit brings about such a complete unity between Christ and his members that St. Paul compares it to the unity of "one flesh": "For no man ever hates his own flesh, but nourishes and cherishes it, as Christ does the church, because we are members of his body. 'For this reason a man shall leave his father and mother and be joined to his wife, and the two shall become one.' This is a great mystery, and I mean in reference to Christ and the church" (Eph 5:29–32). Under normal circumstances, we receive the grace of the Holy Spirit most profoundly through the sensible signs, or sacraments, that mediate to us the power of Christ's cross. St. Paul connects the sacraments to the crucifixion: "Do you not know that all of us who have been baptized into Christ Jesus were baptized into his death?" (Rom 6:3). Since baptism unites us with Christ's death on the cross, it also leads us to share in his resurrection. The Holy Spirit forms Christ's Mystical Body primarily through sacramental grace.

The unity of the Mystical Body should not give the impression that there is no distinctiveness within the Body. Christian life can be either primarily active or primarily contemplative. The active life consists in direct service to others; the contemplative life, in prayer. Most Christians experience both forms of life at various times, although some devote their lives in a special way to the contemplative life. The Holy Spirit also gives to some Christians miraculous graces, such as prophecy or speaking in tongues. Within the Church herself, Christians exercise different duties. St. Thomas writes that "even as in the order of natural things, perfection, which in God is simple and uniform, is not to be found in the created universe except in a multiform and manifold manner, so too, the fulness of grace, which is centered in Christ as head, flows forth to His members in various ways, for the perfecting of the body of the Church" (2-2, q.183, a.2). Although God calls all Christians to charity, it belongs to the perfection of the Church to have a rich diversity among her members, so that each member might serve the others in accord with Christ's example. This mutual service is not an end in itself, but rather aims at the perfection, by grace, of the virtuous life in each member and of the entire Body.

Given this mutuality, we can understand the distinct contributions of the members of religious life, who consecrate themselves to God by vows of poverty, chastity, and obedience, and of the ordained ministry, which includes deacons, priests, and bishops. The evangelical counsels of poverty, chastity, and obedience are shorter and faster paths up the mountain of holiness. Nonetheless, the standard of holiness is the same for all the baptized: "The perfection of the Christian life consists radically in charity" (2-2, q.184, a.1). Every human being is called to this perfection. The Second Vatican Council described this reality as the "universal call to holiness."

The true diversity of the Church comes largely from how her members, by sacramental grace, live out the virtues actively and through contemplative prayer. Not all Christians are called to religious life or holy orders, or to enjoy the gifts of prophecy or tongues. But all Christians are called to be saints. Each saint manifests charity differently; the resulting tapestry, nourished by sacramental grace, is Christ's Mystical Body. Turning now to the sacraments, we will see first that sacraments are not merely symbolic but actually change us by conforming us to Christ. Secondly, we will discuss each of the sacraments individually.

Purpose of the Sacraments

Human beings depend upon sense experience for acquiring knowledge. In establishing his Church, therefore, Christ the teacher instituted sacraments as *sensible signs.* Sacraments are sensible signs that, by the power of God, *cause the spiritual change that they signify.* The New Testament makes clear that Christ instituted sacraments and that these sacraments change us spiritually.

For example, in the risen Lord's words to the apostles in the Gospel of John we find an indication of the sacraments of penance and holy orders: "Jesus said to them again, 'Peace be with you. As the Father has sent me, even so I send you.' And when he had said this, he breathed on them, and said to them, 'Receive the Holy Spirit. If you forgive the sins of any, they are forgiven; if you retain the sins of any, they are retained'" (Jn 20:21–23). Jesus' words change the apostles, who are now sent to act *in persona Christi,* in the Person of Christ. The apostles, through the gift of the Holy Spirit, will change others by the authority to forgive sins. God alone can forgive sins, but he has chosen to do so sacramentally through the apostles and their successors.

Similarly, in his conversation with the Pharisee Nicodemus, Jesus explains that baptism changes human beings spiritually. Jesus tells Nicodemus, "Truly, truly, I say to you, unless one is born of water and the Spirit, he cannot enter the kingdom of God. That which is born of the flesh is flesh, and that which is born of the Spirit is spirit" (Jn 3:5–6). Although baptism does not cause one to re-emerge from the womb, baptism causes a new birth, because it changes the recipient by healing the soul and making the person a sharer in the divine friendship. Through baptism, God makes us children of God who can enter the kingdom of God. As 1 Peter succinctly states, "Baptism . . . now saves you" (3:21).

Jesus makes the same point about the Eucharist. The Eucharist will change those who receive it in faith by giving them eternal life:

> Truly, truly, I say to you, unless you eat the flesh of the Son of man and drink his blood, you have no life in you; he who eats my flesh and drinks my blood has eternal life, and I will raise him up at the last day. For my flesh is food indeed, and my blood is drink indeed. He who eats my flesh and drinks my blood abides in me, and I in him. As the living Father sent me, and I live because of the Father, so he who eats me will live because of me. (Jn 6:53–57)

Many of those who were following Jesus took offense at these words. Jesus, rather than modifying his words, allows those who were offended to leave him; he affirms that his body and blood in the Eucharist convey the divine life. Yet it is not enough to know what the Eucharist is and does. Partaking in the Eucharist without love is an offense against the Mystical Body, a failure to love Christ in his members: "Let a man examine himself, and so eat of the bread and drink of the cup. For any one who eats and drinks without discerning the body eats and drinks judgment upon himself" (1 Cor 11:28–29).

Like the Incarnation, the sacraments are specially adapted to the human condition. As the Christmas liturgy states, "in Jesus Christ we see the invisible God made visible and so are caught up in the love of God whom we cannot see." We are embodied spirits who experience the world through our senses of seeing, hearing, smelling, tasting, and touching. The Incarnation makes God perceivable by us: "That which was from the beginning, which we have heard, which we have seen with our eyes, which we have looked upon and touched with our hands, concerning the word of life" (1 Jn 1:1). The Word continues his physical presence among us through the sacraments. In the sacraments, the invisible grace of God is manifested under physical signs. Through the sacraments, we remain embodied souls while we ascend into the spiritual existence of "partakers of the divine nature" (2 Pet 1:4).

The sacraments of the new law are therefore the instruments through which Christ himself causes and deepens the "new creation" that enables us to enjoy friendship with God. The sacraments of the new law "contain" grace not because grace is a spatial reality (on the contrary), but because they cause the divine life in us. Just as Christ's humanity is the "instrument" through which his divinity works our salvation in the world, the sacraments are related to Christ's humanity as the instruments by which he, our savior and teacher, shares with human beings the new life that he has won for us. St. Thomas affirms that the Church "is built on faith and the sacraments of faith" (3, q.64, a.2, ad 2). Whereas in heaven we will no longer need the sacraments or the visible Church, the visible Church and the sacraments both correspond to the concrete, historical character of this present life. The sacraments thus cannot be understood apart from the Church in her nature as one, holy, catholic (universal), and apostolic. Christ's Mystical Body takes shape as, through the sacraments, Christ the Head restores and perfects his members by applying the power of his cross to all aspects of our lives, converting our self-centered lives into the image of his self-giving charity.

The Individual Sacraments

The first sacrament, baptism, unites us with Christ's cross and resurrection. We are buried with Christ (incorporated into his sacrificial self-offering) so that we might rise with him. By removing our sin through our new participation in Christ's cross, baptism causes the infusion of the grace of the Holy Spirit that establishes within us the bond of divine friendship. This divine friendship makes us Israel's Temple fulfilled. Transformed by this new life, the believer receives the indwelling of the Trinity and is established in habitual grace—the grace of being a child of God (divine filiation).

Habitual grace expresses the reality that the Holy Spirit has truly changed the person's soul, so that his soul is now a new creation. St. Paul writes that "if anyone is in Christ, he is a new creation; the old has passed away, behold, the new has come" (2 Cor 5:17) and "For neither circumcision counts for anything, nor uncircumcision, but a new creation" (Gal 6:15). In baptism, the believer is given the relationship of friendship with God that fulfills the prophesy of Ezekiel: "And I will give them one heart, and put a new spirit within them; I will take the stony heart out of their flesh and give them a heart of flesh, that they may walk in my statutes and keep my ordinances and obey them; and they shall be my people, and I will be their God" (Ezek 11:19–20).

If baptism causes the divine life in us, we might think that people should be baptized against their will, so that everyone might benefit. St. Thomas strongly rejects this idea. In the case of Jewish children, for example, he notes that unless the child has reached the age of full possession of free will and freely chooses baptism, baptizing a Jewish child would be sinful. He also rejects forced baptism of adults as a violation of free will. Under normal circumstances, baptism is necessary for entering into the new friendship with God in Jesus Christ—the friendship that is our salvation. Yet God's power "is not tied to the visible sacraments" (3, q.68, a.2). Christ promised paradise to the thief on the cross, although the thief had no opportunity for water baptism. Nevertheless, when the resurrected Christ later appeared to his disciples he instructed them: "Go into all the world and preach the gospel to the whole creation. He who believes and is baptized will be saved; but he who does not believe will be condemned" (Mk 16:15–16).

A different case is the baptism of children with the permission of their parents and the baptism of those who never have the opportunity to exercise free will because they suffer from birth from insanity or a mental handicap. The various forms of insanity and mental handicaps are not a deformity of the soul, but a deformity of the body (3, q.68, a.12, ad 2). Christ calls the mentally disabled to be united to himself. Explaining the baptism of infants, St. Thomas remarks that "as the child while in the mother's womb receives nourishment not independently, but through the nourishment of its mother, so also children before the use of reason, being as it were in the womb of their mother the Church, receive salvation not by their own act, but by the act of the Church" (3, q.68, a.9, ad 1). This can be understood once one recognizes that the Church is truly a Mystical Body through whom we receive spiritual nourishment. The baptism of infants, who contribute nothing to the sacrament, exemplifies as well that salvation is always a free, unearned gift from God.

Baptism changes a person *permanently*. It "marks" or "seals" the recipient in the image or "character" of Christ. Through baptism (and later confirmation), the *imago dei* in us becomes permanently conformed to Christ's cross and enabled to participate in his self-offering on the cross. We become like Christ, another Christ. St. Augustine preached to the baptized, "Let us rejoice and give thanks, for we have become not only Christians, but Christ. . . . Marvel and rejoice: we have become Christ!" (*Tractates on John* 21, 8). We thus share in his fulfillment of the Mosaic Law and inauguration of the new law in his priestly, prophetic, and kingly offices. Baptism grants all the baptized "a spiritual priesthood for offering spiritual sacrifices" (3, q.82, a.1, ad 2; cf. 1 Peter 2:5). The entire Mystical Body brings its spiritual sacrifices to be offered to God in the Eucharist.

What does confirmation add to baptism? St. Thomas associates it with giving the baptized the strength to share in Christ's sacrifice by proclaiming their faith by words and deeds in public. As does baptism, confirmation stamps a lasting image of Christ on the recipient. The strength to undergo martyrdom is secured by confirmation. The apostles, after Christ's resurrection and ascension, were made strong to preach the good news and risk martyrdom when the Holy Spirit "confirmed" them at Pentecost (3, q.72, a.2, ad 1). In discussing confirmation, St. Thomas notes that Christ had the authority to institute a sacrament simply by promising it. He promises the sacrament of confirmation in John 16:7: "If I do not go away, the Counselor [Holy Spirit] will not come to you; but if I go, I will send him to you." Christ sends the Holy Spirit fully upon his disciples after his resurrection and ascension.

The greatest sacrament is the Eucharist. St. Thomas considers the Eucharist the greatest sacrament for three reasons: first, the Eucharist contains Christ *substantially* rather than simply sharing in Christ's power instrumentally; second, the other sacraments are ordered to the Eucharist; and, third, the Eucharist is the highest point of our worship. In giving himself to us in the Eucharist, Christ draws believers into the most intimate friendship of self-giving love with himself. We are drawn into participating in Christ's eternal sacrifice. The Eucharist is the sacrament in which the salvation we described in the last chapter is fully manifested: we share perfectly in Christ's sacrifice as members of his Mystical Body. In the Eucharist, Christ cannot be separated from his body, the Church. The whole Christ, head and members, is present in the Eucharist.

The Eucharist *is* Christ "under the sacramental species": as St. Thomas states, "we eat Christ," who nourishes us spiritually (3, q.73, a.5, ad 1). In light of the Catholic Church's formal declaration in 1215 of the doctrine of transubstantiation, St. Thomas explores how the sacramental species (bread and wine) are substantially changed so that under the sensible appearance—taste, smell, touch, sight—of bread and wine, not bread and wine but rather Christ's body, blood, soul, and divinity are substantially present. Given Christ's substantial presence in the Eucharist, the Eucharist is the sacrament that most perfectly signifies Christ's Mystical Body. For this reason Christ instituted the sacrament of the Eucharist on the eve of his crucifixion "because last words, chiefly such as are spoken by departing friends, are committed most deeply to memory; since then especially affection for friends is more enkindled, and the things which affect us most are impressed the deepest in the soul" (3, q.73, a.5). In partaking in the Eucharist, we enjoy fully the intimate friendship, or intimate communion, with Christ that constitutes our new existence as members of Christ's Mystical Body and sharers in the sacrificial worship of the fulfilled Temple.

The Eucharist is thus a "sacrifice," as St. Thomas points out, not merely because it re-presents Christ's sacrifice, but also because it brings about our fullest sharing in the power of Christ's sacrifice. It is both a sacrifice and a meal, a sacrificial meal in which those who eat *enter into* the sacrifice. It does not repeat Christ's once-and-for-all sacrifice; rather, it enables us to *share in* Christ's perfect sacrifice. Since Christ's sacrifice is perfect it remains in act. It does not fade with time, as would a painting of the cross. The fact that Christ's sacrifice is one and perfect is what enables it to be re-presented in each Eucharist. The Epistle to the Hebrews captures this dynamism of the Eucharist: "[Jesus Christ] always lives to make intercession for them" (7:25), and "he did this once for all when he offered up himself" (7:27). In the biblical language, Christ's sacrifice is both "always" and "once for all." Each celebration of the Eucharist enables us to enter into the eternal offering of the Son to the Father. As members of Christ's body, we join with our Head and are incorporated into the sacrifice that Christ offered upon the cross. By sharing in his sacrifice, as we saw in the last chapter, we share in the forgiveness of sins and outpouring of the Holy Spirit that his sacrificial love brought about for humankind.

In the sacrament of penance, Christ restores and strengthens in us the intimate friendship with him that we had gained through baptism, and had weakened or lost through sin. Sometimes people ask why, under normal circumstances, we should not simply repent and be forgiven directly by Christ. Why should a priest be involved? The answer is that salvation is not an individualistic transaction between a person and Christ, but rather is caught up in the salvation of the whole Mystical Body and does not occur apart from it. It is true that forgiveness can be received outside the sacrament when there is an implicit desire to receive the sacrament. Confession of sins to a priest, however, is a necessary element of the sacrament, because of the authority the priest receives in ordination to bestow the divine gifts. Once forgiven, the repentant sinner is fully restored to the communion of the Mystical Body by performing an act of penance. Since sin wounds Christ's Mystical Body, it is fitting that the forgiven sinner make a spiritual or physical sacrifice as part of fully participating once again in the sacrifice by which Christ restored the world.

Some people also question why, if Christ is acting so powerfully through the sacraments to transform, strengthen, and nourish us, Catholics appear to be just as much sinners as everybody else. Simply put, the sacraments cannot prevent us from falling back into sin, since our wills remain weakened. On the other hand, our wills are strengthened insofar as we participate in Christ's sacrifice, and the sacraments, when we have recourse to them, fuel our continual *conversion*. Received with a spirit of faith and repentance, the sacrament of penance restores the person to full life in Christ.

As shown by the sacrament of penance (along with the penitential acts that belong to the liturgy), Christ's Mystical Body on earth is a place of healing and forgiveness, just as Christ's words and deeds on earth were aimed at healing and forgiving sinners. Christ's Mystical Body is holy—otherwise it could not be filled with grace or *be* his Body—yet, as the sacrament of penance indicates, the members of the Body are sinners who individually and collectively need the grace of continual repentance. The sacrament of penance turns us from pride to conversion and healing. This change is ongoing throughout our lives; it characterizes our communal life as members of Christ's Body.

The sacrament of the anointing of the sick, or extreme unction, is another way that Christ sacramentally unites his members with his victorious cross. Most sickness is not directly caused by sin, although some sins, such as drunkenness or illicit drug use, can cause sickness in our bodies. As we saw, however, all physical sickness can ultimately be traced back to the corruption caused by original sin. The last sacrament that we experience is therefore an anointing of our mortally ill bodies—in mortal illness we experience profoundly the penalty of sin. The sacrament of the anointing of our body heals the underlying spiritual cause of our mortal suffering. It is a sacrament because the anointing, through the power of Christ's cross, prepares our body for spiritual glorification.

The sacrament of marriage conforms the man and woman to the image of Christ and the Church (the image of the Mystical Body) as they enter into a mutually self-giving covenant ordered to fruitful love. Explaining the indissolubility of marriage, St. Thomas notes that "the greater that friendship is, the more solid and long-lasting will it be. Now, there seems to be the greatest friendship between husband and wife, for they are united not only in the act of fleshly union . . . but also in the partnership of the whole range of domestic activity" (*Summa contra Gentiles* 3, 123). The sacrament of marriage transforms natural marriage, already an exalted form of friendship, by giving the couple the grace to give themselves fully to each other. The self-giving love of marriage is intrinsically ordered toward the *welcoming of other selves*—that is, the having and raising of children. Thus, as St. Thomas points out, any union that deliberately excludes the intention to have children cannot be a marriage. The sacrament strengthens the couple in their efforts to ensure that Christ's self-giving love is embodied by every act of the married couple. Through his presence in the sacrament of marriage—a presence symbolized by the blessing of the union by a priest—Christ transforms the human friendship that is at the heart of the transmission of life.

The sacrament of orders comes last in our discussion because of its special role in uniting the divine gifts that Christ gives us, namely, his sacraments and teachings. By understanding the sacrament of orders, we can grasp how the Church's sacraments are intrinsically related to the Church's apostolic task of teaching the content of Christ's good news for all people. Christ's sacramental presence is always united to the truth he teaches.

As we have seen, the apostles were sent directly by Christ, who breathed the Holy Spirit upon them and charged them to go forth to "all nations, baptizing them in the name of the Father and of the Son and of the Holy Spirit, teaching them to observe all that I have commanded you" (Mt 28:19–20). By laying on hands, the apostles gave this sacrament to their successors, the bishops. St. Paul reminds his beloved Timothy, whom he had chosen as a successor: "Do not neglect the gift you have, which was given you by prophetic utterance when the elders laid their hands upon you" (1 Tim 4:14).

The sacrament of orders bestows on the recipient not only the power to perform the sacraments, but also the power to preach the true content of faith (all that Christ has commanded). Recall that the purpose of the sacraments is to unite Christ's members in his wisdom and sacrificial love. Christ teaches, "If you keep my commandments, you will abide in my love, just as I have kept my Father's commandments and abide in his love" (Jn 15:10). Abiding in his love depends upon knowing what his commandments truly are. Christ gave the sacrament of orders so that his Church might be unified in truth. When disputes arise, the pope and the bishops united with the pope establish the unity in truth that Christ has willed to give his Church. All generations thus can come to know the truth that Christ teaches (a truth that is known more profoundly as doctrine develops in the Church) and to live the truth in love.

St. Thomas is well aware that the pope's authority, and that of the other bishops, is not something that they merit by their goodness. He criticizes harshly some bishops of his day who "are so eager for and occupied with temporal gain that they neglect the spiritual welfare of their subjects" (*Commentary on John*, chap. 2, lecture 2). Their authority flows not from their merit but from Christ's love and gift. While every sin wounds the Church, still, the Church's holiness is not undone by their personal failings. The sacraments and teachings convey the holiness of Christ, who is "the way, the truth, and the life; no one comes to the Father, but by me" (Jn 14:6).

Although the Church is the community of the Holy Spirit, and in this sense fundamentally an interior communion, the Holy Spirit preserves the Church's unity of faith through the visible ministry of the bishops, led by the bishop of Rome. The Holy Spirit works through the apostolic ministry. As St. Thomas notes, for example, the Church's creeds are to be believed because "the universal Church cannot err, since she is governed by the Holy Spirit, who is the Spirit of truth: for such was our Lord's promise to His disciples (Jn 16:13)" (2-2, q.1, a.9). The authority behind the Church's creed is thus the Holy Spirit. Yet the authority to publish creeds belongs to the pope, who "is empowered to decide matters of faith finally, so that they may be held by all with unshaken faith" (2-2, q.1, a.10).

This visible unity under the guidance of the Holy Spirit, working through the ordained ministers, ensures that the faithful truly receive Christ in the teachings and sacraments of the Church. Jesus promised this ongoing relationship: "If you continue in my word, you are truly my disciples, and you will know the truth, and the truth will make you free" (Jn 8:31–32). The teachings of the Church—teachings inspired by the Holy Spirit, who, as Jesus says, will "teach you all things" (Jn 14:26), and affirmed by the bishops in accord with their sacramental authority—belong to the sacramental path by which we are led to union in Christ with the Trinity. Our way to submit to Christ is by submitting, in charity, to the teachings of his apostles and their episcopal successors. As Jesus said to his apostles, "he who hears you hears me, and he who rejects you rejects me, and he who rejects me rejects him who sent me" (Luke 10:16).

And so, Christian life together is a gift. To belong, whether visibly or invisibly, to the Mystical Body of Christ, the People of God, means receiving everything from the Trinity's wisdom and love. This is why the apostles and their successors make decisions for the whole Body about Christian faith and morality, without violating the free will of believers. Christians freely choose a life characterized by *receiving*. It could not be any other way, since to follow Jesus, we must allow ourselves to be guided by him. We learn that he is trustworthy by experiencing, in faith, that he is truly the good shepherd who leads us further into the depths of love, the more we allow ourselves to follow him (Jn 10:11). Indeed, as St. Thomas points out, if we choose to hold some of the Church's teachings but reject others, we have actually lost our freedom, the freedom of the follower of Christ. True freedom is found in recognizing the gift-character of the Mystical Body. This is the great mystery of the Church: in giving ourselves out of love, we *receive* our true selves. As the risen Lord tells the church in Pergamum: "To him who conquers I will give some of the hidden manna, and I will give him a white stone, with a new name written on the stone which no one knows except him who receives it" (Rev 2:17).

CHAPTER EIGHT

ETERNAL LIFE

We have all heard people describe what they would like eternal life to be like. Some people are sure that heaven could not be complete without books. Some people want lots of sensual pleasures. Others want their dogs. When a professional athlete dies, the eulogies always assure us that he or she is now playing on the big baseball field in the sky, or hitting from the first tee somewhere near the Pearly Gates.

Jesus puts a damper upon such imaginings. For those who want books, he teaches that in heaven we will know God as he is, so books will hardly be necessary. For those who want sensual pleasures, he states that "in the resurrection they neither marry nor are given in marriage, but are like angels in heaven" (Mt 22:30). For those who want their dogs, he gives no particular encouragement!

Yet the New Testament gives us a number of hints about eternal life. In accord with his vocation as a theologian, St. Thomas seeks to understand these hints. He understands eternal life not as a flight from history, but as the liturgical *consummation* of history. Human history will not be fulfilled until, as the prophet Isaiah writes, "By myself I have sworn, from my mouth has gone forth in righteousness a word that shall not return: 'To me every knee shall bow, every tongue shall swear'" (Is 45:23). Or as St. Paul describes the end of history: "For we shall all stand before the judgment seat of God" (Rom 14:10).

Hell

Before discussing heaven, it is necessary to discuss heaven's opposite. God has called us to union with him in heaven, but we are free to reject that call. As we saw in our earlier section on God's providence, this is known as reprobation or damnation. Those who choose to exclude themselves from God's presence lose their true good. Nonetheless, Christ is the Head of all humankind. The damned are permanently separated from the Mystical Body—which is a communion constituted by charity—because in their freedom, they have permanently chosen selfish love over the self-giving love of Christ. Yet the damned remain related to the Mystical Body through the justice of the judgment rendered by Christ and the saints. Through this justice even the damned belong to the perfect consummation of all things. The words of the Psalmist come true: "How great are thy works, O Lord! Thy thoughts are very deep! The dull man cannot know, the stupid cannot understand this: that, though the wicked sprout like grass and all evildoers flourish, they are doomed to destruction for ever, but thou, O Lord, art on high for ever" (Ps 92:5–8).

As the judge, who judges by the measuring-rod of charity, Christ sums up all things in relation to his charity. The saints, who share in Christ's judiciary power by sharing in his cross, will judge by consenting to Christ's judgment. St. Paul reminds the Corinthian Christians, "Do you not know that the saints will judge the world?" (1 Cor 6:2). Because of their humble charity, the saints are able to judge the damned with perfect justice. The seer of the Book of Revelation describes this unity of the saints with Christ their Head in judging:

> Then I saw heaven opened, and behold, a white horse! He who sat upon it is called Faithful and True, and in righteousness he judges and makes war. His eyes are like a flame of fire, and on his head are many diadems; and he has a name inscribed which no one knows but himself. He is clad in a robe dipped in blood, and the name by which he is called is The Word of God. And the armies of heaven, arrayed in fine linen, white and pure, followed him on white horses. From his mouth issues a sharp sword with which to smite the nations, and he will rule them with a rod of iron; he will tread the wine press of the fury of the wrath of God the Almighty. (Rev 19:11–16)

The two-edged sword in the mouth of the Word of God is his cross, which is mercy for those who receive it and justice for those who reject it. Since the saints share the divine love, the knowledge of the suffering of the damned does not impede their happiness, because like God they love each creature in accord with its degree of goodness.

But how can this be? How can anyone rejoice when another is suffering? Many people are unable to imagine how the saints could rejoice if even one human being, or one fallen angel, is suffering forever in hell. Although the Church has taught that hell exists, it is sometimes remarked that the Church has never declared that any particular human being is in hell. Yet the Church has affirmed consistently that Satan, formerly among the highest angels, is everlastingly in hell. Hell is populated by at least one rational creature—who was once a beautiful angel! Even so, St. Thomas, with Holy Scripture, teaches that the blessed will rejoice. Why?

The answer is that charity involves a desire for justice. Since the fulfillment of justice is a great good, the saints rejoice in it. As we grow in charity, we become more sensitive to injustice and yearn ever more deeply for the fulfillment of justice. The Psalmist, looking around himself and finding the same evildoing that we find today, implores, "O Lord, how long shall the wicked, how long shall the wicked exult? They pour out their arrogant words, they boast, all the evildoers. They crush thy people, O Lord, and afflict thy heritage. They slay the widow and the sojourner, and murder the fatherless; and they say, 'The Lord does not see; the God of Jacob does not perceive'" (Ps 94:3–7). The saints share the desire of the Psalmist.

By taking our sins upon himself, Jesus fulfills all justice. Not all people will choose to embrace the justice he offers. The exulting and boasting of the wicked continue until the end of time, and although some of us will repent and embrace God's mercy in Jesus Christ, others of us will not repent. For this reason, even though Jesus has established justice, he commands that his followers, like the Psalmist, hunger for justice, in themselves and in others: "Blessed are those who hunger and thirst for righteousness, for they shall be satisfied" (Mt 5:6). St. John, writing to the first Christians, urges them to pursue justice: "For this is the message which you have heard from the beginning, that we should love one another, and not be like Cain who was of the evil one and murdered his brother" (1 Jn 3:11–12). As the seer of the Book of Revelation depicts the final judgment, "Then I saw a great white throne and him who sat upon it. . . . And I saw the dead, great and small, standing before the throne, and books were opened. Also another book was opened, which is the book of life. And the dead were judged by what was written in the books, by what they had done. . . . and if any one's name was not found written in the book of life, he was thrown into the lake of fire" (Rev 20:11–12, 15; cf. Mt 25:31–46). The hunger and thirst for justice will be satisfied, although the saints depend upon Christ, not upon themselves, for salvation: "because I [Christ] live, you will live also" (Jn 14:19).

Hell may nonetheless still seem too great a price for the establishment of God's providential and merciful justice. Since charity in us is imperfect, we at times sinfully wish evil upon others. Hell can seem merely another act of human vengeance, which is almost inevitably colored by lack of charity and by the desire to see our enemies put down. When someone wrongs us, we often ignore Jesus' command to "turn the other cheek" and forgive. How common it is instead to seek hate-filled revenge.

Thus, when we imagine the justice that characterizes eternal life, we have trouble realizing that hell is charitable justice, not the revenge that we would uncharitably like God to take upon our enemies. As St. Peter teaches, God wishes that "all should reach repentance" (2 Pet 3:9). God, in Jesus Christ, has forgiven each person who is in hell, but they have rejected that forgiveness. Hell is chosen by people. As some have put it, the door to hell is only locked on the inside; people have freely chosen to exclude themselves from the heavenly banquet. The only way to understand hell is to realize that people's final rejection of God's love does not mean that they thereby break away from the *order* of his love. Rather, as St. Thomas shows, this order of love manifests itself in justice. Justice implies punishment, a suffering on the part of the unjust person for the sufferings he or she has caused. The unjust can only experience the divine presence as punishment. In the order of justice, those who reject God's love experience God's presence as wrath, since his presence (as judge) continually inflames their anguish—the anguish of having lost, through their own hateful distortion, the good intended for them.

Heaven

The Book of Revelation is a main source for St. Thomas's understanding of eternal life. The seer of the Book of Revelation weaves together prophetic images from the Old Testament to depict the new creation:

> Then I saw a new heaven and a new earth; for the first heaven and
> the first earth had passed away, and the sea [disorder] was no more.
> And I saw the holy city, new Jerusalem, coming down out of heaven
> from God, prepared as a bride adorned for her husband; and I heard
> a great voice from the throne saying, "Behold, the dwelling of God
> is with men. He will dwell with them, and they shall be his people,
> and God himself will be with them; he will wipe away every tear
> from their eyes, and death shall be no more, neither shall there be
> mourning nor crying nor pain any more, for the former things have
> passed away." (Rev 21:1–4)

At the end of time, the Mystical Body will be consummated by the God-
man's direct presence, his Second Coming. Just as Israel's Temple was to
be the dwelling-place of God's name, so Christ's presence will inaugu-
rate and enliven the new creation at the final judgment. As the seer of the
Book of Revelation states, "I saw no temple in the city, for its temple is the
Lord God the Almighty and the Lamb. And the city has no need of sun
or moon to shine upon it, for the glory of God is its light, and its lamp is
the Lamb" (Rev 21:22–23). In the fulfilled Mystical Body, our relationship (as members of Christ) to the Trinity will be so intimate that the
Trinity will be the Temple in which we dwell.

If the Trinity will be the Temple, does this mean that there will be
no need for the material cosmos? Is the next life an "otherworldly" arena
that will include only human beings, and nothing else belonging to the
cosmos? On the contrary, the new creation will be a new creation of the
entire cosmos. The cosmos is not a vast evolutionary tree to be chopped
down after God has plucked the fruit, namely, human beings. Rather, as
St. Thomas says, human beings naturally love the whole created order,
since we belong to it. It is fitting that God should transform the entire
material creation together. In the Book of Revelation, the angel who proclaims that the redemptive "mystery of God, as he announced to his servants the prophets, should be fulfilled," swears by the *Creator,* "him who
lives for ever and ever, who created heaven and what is in it, the earth and
what is in it, and the sea and what is in it" (Rev 10:5–7). The Creator will
transform everything together.

Obviously, in the transformed cosmos, many things will be different.
There will be no begetting of new life or corruption of old life, or any of
the movements connected with begetting and corruption. These movements belonged to the way in which God sustained the vitality of creation

as it moved toward its goal, and will cease once the goal has been reached. Every element of the cosmos will be present and transformed in the new creation. Scripture does not say in what way the material elements will remain, but in some form they will be present. The main point is that our bodies will not be the only material elements in heaven. Heaven truly is the renewal and transformation of the whole cosmos.

What will our bodies be like in heaven? St. Paul encourages the Corinthians, who asked this question, by comparing death to the sowing of a seed: "So it is with the resurrection of the body. What is sown is perishable, what is raised is imperishable. It is sown in dishonor, it is raised in glory. It is sown in weakness, it is raised in power. It is sown a physical body, it is raised a spiritual body" (1 Cor 15:42–44). Jesus promises that "in my Father's house are many rooms; if it were not so, would I have told you that I go to prepare a place for you?" (Jn 14:2). Just as Jesus risen is the same man who was born in Nazareth and died on the Cross, the resurrected bodies will be the same bodies, and yet they will not possess the defects caused by original sin, such as imperfect development, chronic disease, or decrepitude. God will restore human bodies to how they would have been without original sin. This will not mean that all bodies will look alike, but that each body will reach its natural perfection. Moreover, the bodies of the blessed will not only be restored, but also perfected. According to St. Thomas, the bodies of the blessed, like Christ's glorified body, will be perfected by at least four qualities: impassibility (incorruptibility), subtlety (harmony), agility (movement), and clarity (light). Each of these qualities removes impediments to the body's truly participating in the glorified soul's everlasting worship.

Impassibility begins with the fact that the body will be perfectly ruled by the soul. Through the restoration of due order, God will govern the soul, and the soul will govern the body. In heaven, this order will be perfected so as to be incorruptible. The soul's governance of the body means that the body will no longer be subject to disordered passions and physical corruption, although the body will retain sensation. Indeed, in heaven all the senses will be perfectly in act, in conformity with the glory of the soul. In short, the glorified body, no less than the glorified soul, will participate eternally in the heavenly liturgy, without fear of corrupting or falling away. In eternal life, physical signs of virtue, such as the wounds received by Christ, may remain as beautiful marks of spiritual victory, but they will no longer retain the aspect of corruptibility or invite further decay.

The other qualities—subtlety, agility, and clarity—enable the body to share fully in the spiritual worship of heaven. As St. Paul teaches, the glorified body is a new creation: "It is sown a physical body, it is raised a spiritual body" (1 Cor 15:44). Subtlety is the ability of the body to move freely. This does not mean that glorified bodies take on the power of spiritual substances and no longer occupy any space. Rather, the subtlety of glorified bodies enables them to move together in harmony, without causing disturbance or friction. There will be no crowding in the divine liturgy of heaven, no matter how many resurrected human beings are present.

Agility refers to the fact that the glorified body will perfectly reflect its glorified soul's spiritual movements of praise. The praise offered bodily by the blessed in heaven will not be laborious or burdensome, and so they will not tire out and need to rest. Although the soul's beatific communion with God will be unchanging, the blessed in heaven will not be still, but will move bodily. St. Thomas states that the saints' "vision may be refreshed by the beauty of the variety of creatures, in which God's wisdom will shine forth with great evidence: for sense can only perceive that which is present, although glorified bodies can perceive from a greater distance than non-glorified bodies" (*Commentary on the Sentences,* book 4, distinction 44, q.2, a.3, qla.2 [minor question 2]; cf. Supplement to the *Summa Theologiae,* q.84, a.2). Movement will enable the saints to see, with their bodily eyes, the full panorama of the glory of God's material creation. In Dante's *Paradiso,* the beatified souls are depicted as dancing.

In explaining the saints' bodily clarity, St. Thomas cites Wisdom 3:7, which is about the righteous after death: "In the time of their visitation they will shine forth, and will run like sparks through the stubble." This clarity will not erase the body's natural color, but will make the body resplendent, in proportion to the soul's degree of charity. St. Matthew describes Jesus' transfiguration: "his face shone like the sun, and his garments became white as light" (Mt 17:2). Like Christ, the glorified bodies of the saints will be resplendent. As Jesus depicts the final judgment: "The Son of man will send his angels, and they will gather out of his kingdom all causes of sin and all evildoers, and throw them into the furnace of fire; there men will weep and gnash their teeth. Then the righteous will shine like the sun in the kingdom of their Father" (Mt 13:41–43).

In short, marked by harmony, movement, and light, the bodily communion of the saints within the consummated Mystical Body of Christ will truly fulfill the promise of the earthly liturgy. Human beings will rejoice in seeing, with their bodily eyes, Christ and the other saints. Human beings will also rejoice in the wondrous beauty of the transformed world. Heaven will be suffused by those delights of the body that express the soul's blessedness.

This bodily glorification flows from the saints' perfect spiritual communion with the Trinity. Through the beatific vision, in which we see God face to face and know him as he is, the faculties that differentiate human beings from other animals—namely, the ability to know and love God, and all things in relation to God—are transformed, elevated, and perfected. The beatific vision constitutes the ultimate sharing in Christ's sacrifice of praise. Human knowing and loving will be taken into the knowing and loving that characterizes the life of the divine Persons. Human beings will thus participate in the dynamic communion of the divine Persons and truly "see" (by intellectual vision) the essence of God, which subsists in the divine Persons.

This experience, while anticipated in the eucharistic liturgy in which the Church receives communion in the God-man, will go infinitely beyond the liturgy of the present state. St. Thomas repeatedly returns to the Johannine passages, "We shall see him as he is" (1 Jn 3:2) and "This is eternal life, that they know Thee the only true God" (Jn 17:3). Similarly the author of the Book of Revelation states, "There shall no more be anything accursed, but the throne of God and of the Lamb shall be in it [the new Jerusalem], and his servants shall worship him; they shall see his face, and his name shall be on their foreheads" (Rev 22:3–4). The beatific vision is perfect sharing or participating in the nature of the triune God, who is pure spirit. The vision is profound intimacy and unfathomable friendship with God.

St. Thomas explains that the analogy of vision can be misleading. When we see corporeal things, their likeness is present in our mind, but not their essence. God cannot be seen in this way, because no bodily likeness can convey the incorporeal (pure spirit). Moreover, no human concept can convey God's essence. The essence of God is his existence, which is not true for any created form, and thus cannot be grasped in a human concept. No concept can grasp God's essence, because the concept is limited, while God is unlimited.

Indeed, if we were to say that the beatific vision takes place through a created concept, then the vision could not be a true vision of God. Instead, God joins himself to the created intellect, in an inexpressibly intimate fashion. The interior presence of God transforms, elevates, and perfects the human intellect to "see" God. God makes himself (unmediated by any concept) the object of the glorified soul's intellectual vision. Yet, since only the infinite can exhaustively grasp the infinite, God is properly said to be "incomprehensible" even for the blessed. St. Thomas affirms, "God is called incomprehensible not because anything of Him is not seen; but because He is not seen as perfectly as He is capable of being seen" (1, q.12, a.7, ad 2). In the worship that characterizes the state of glory, God is known but remains a mystery.

Recall from our earlier discussion that the interior presence of God in the soul causes the light of grace. To know God is natural to God alone. The light of grace—which is consummated in the light of glory—is the gift by which God enables our minds to know him. Since grace is the transformation of the creature's soul, grace is (as it exists in the creature) created, although it is the work of the uncreated Trinity. The point is simply that by grace, the creature does not *become* the Creator, but rather becomes a new creation, enabled to participate in the trinitarian life. As St. Paul says, "For all who are led by the Spirit of God are sons of God" (Rom 8:14). In heaven, the light of grace (an intellectual light, elevating our souls to know and love God) is perfected by the light of glory, which establishes us permanently in perfect communion with God.

It might be asked, however, whether grace thus constitutes a medium between the soul and God, so that the soul does not really attain direct knowledge of God. St. Thomas explains that the light of glory, elevating the intellect by a kind of "deiformity," or likeness, to see God, is not "a medium in which God is seen, but . . . one by which He is seen; and such a medium does not take away the immediate vision of God" (1, q.12, a.5, ad 2). Since the beatific vision comes about through the elevating of the intellect accomplished by grace, it is also worth noting that more intelligent people are not privileged in the beatific vision. The light of glory elevates and perfects, but does not depend upon, the natural light of the intellect. The light of glory is given by God to human beings without regard to the acuity of their natural intellects. Instead, the degree of *love* that a person possesses determines the degree to which one will know God. The saints are distinguished by their charity. The worship enjoyed by the saints is an exercise not simply of the intellect, but also of the will. In the end, we will be judged by our love.

The beatific vision enjoyed by the individual takes place within the context of the Mystical Body of Christ—there is no individualistic salvation. Since Christ is eternally priest, he remains the source of the light of glory that enlightens the consummated Mystical Body, even if redemption from sin is no longer needed by the saints. As St. Thomas writes, "The Saints who will be in heaven will not need any further expiation by the priesthood of Christ, but having expiated, they will need consummation through Christ Himself, on Whom their glory depends" (3, q.22, a.5). In heaven, the glorious unity of Christ's Mystical Body will be manifested: "The glory which thou hast given me I have given to them, that they may be one even as we are one, I in them and thou in me" (Jn 17:22–23). This glory will be the everlasting marriage of God and man. "Hallelujah! For the Lord our God the Almighty reigns. Let us rejoice and exult and give him the glory, for the marriage of the Lamb has come, and his Bride has made herself ready; it was granted her to be clothed with fine linen, bright and pure" (Rev 19:6–8).

It should be noted that St. Thomas recognizes the existence of purgatory as a final preparation for heaven. Purgatory is the condition after death in which people who are united to Christ in love, though imperfectly, are purified of the remaining inner consequences of their sins so that they might perfectly enjoy Christ's presence in heaven. Not only does purgatory purify remaining character deformations, it also allows the saved to endure any temporal punishment that remains due for their sins. Purgatory is for those who die in a state of grace, that is, united to Christ in faith and charity. All the saved, in fact, require purification, penance, and mortification in order to be fully perfected in Christ. As Jesus teaches, "If any man would come after me, let him deny himself and take up his cross daily and follow me" (Lk 9:23). The lives of the saints teach us that Christians are called to begin self-denial and mortification now, thus living purgatory while in this present life.

Heaven is the consummation of Christ's work, through the Holy Spirit, of reconciling all things. The glorious reality that is heaven does not negate either the Old or the New Covenant. Instead, both are fulfilled by the perfect holiness and perfect worship enjoyed by the glorified human beings and angels in harmony with the renewed cosmos. In Dante's image, heaven is like a beautiful celestial rose, enlivened by the Trinity's supremely active presence and watered by Christ, in which all the saints, like petals, have their glorious place.

CONCLUSION

We have reached the end of our book's journey from the Trinity *to* the Trinity. Nonetheless, our contemplative ascent with the assistance of St. Thomas as a spiritual master should be just beginning. St. Thomas's *Summa Theologiae* is for "beginners" because it teaches us how to ask questions about the mysteries of Christian faith. Jesus our teacher encourages us, "Ask, and it will be given you; seek, and you will find; knock, and it will be opened to you" (Mt 7:7). In the preceding chapters, we have learned about a radically new way of life that has its origins in the wisdom and love of the Trinity, that teaches us how to be people who share in that wisdom and love by faith in Jesus Christ, and that leads us to a beatitude far beyond what we could ever imagine—to a perfect sharing in the divine trinitarian life.

In gaining insight into this radically new way of life, we have also learned some of the practices that enable us to enter into this way of life. Our minds have been purified of false notions of God and creation, and have glimpsed the mysterious font of existence who sustains and guides human history, despite the effects of sin, toward ultimate consummation. We have been led toward a deeper understanding of the context in which our hearts are hungry for happiness, and have learned something of the skills or virtues by which we may attain this deepest and lasting happiness—a happiness that the Holy Spirit himself is drawing us toward through the gifts of supernatural faith, hope, and love. We have contemplated, in his two natures, the Person of Jesus Christ, whose sacrifice, as supreme love, fulfills all justice, heals and restores the image of God within us, and frees us for the grace of the Holy Spirit. We have learned how the teachings and sacraments of the Church are nothing less than Christ's gifts that change us by conforming us to Christ's humility and sacrificial love; we have learned the path that enables our lives, like Christ's, to express the reality that all is divine gift. We have caught a glimpse of the wondrous communion that is the unfathomable happiness of heaven, the celestial rose where we are joined, by a marital bond of love in which we know the divine lover, to the Trinity.

Our book has thus been an invitation to a way of forming minds and hearts in community with others and in communion with the triune God. Every chapter has pointed beyond itself to the source of our questions, the source of our joy in study and contemplation. In conclusion, we can do no more than to continue to ask, to seek, to knock; and to anticipate the coming of our teacher to instruct us with final completeness, as we continue the adventure of risking our lives to follow with humility the truth we have loved. As the seer of the Book of Revelation concludes, "The Spirit and the Bride say, 'Come.' And let him who hears say, 'Come.' And let him who is thirsty come, let him who desires take the water of life without price" (Rev 22:17).

Note on Editions

For quotations from St. Thomas's *Summa Theologiae,* we have used the translation by the Fathers of the English Dominican Province published in 1920 (St. Thomas Aquinas, *Summa Theologica,* 5 vols [Westminster, Md.: Christian Classics, 1981]).

For quotations from the Bible, we have used the Revised Standard Version, Catholic Edition, published in 1966.

For quotations from St. Thomas's *Commentary on the Gospel of Saint John* [Lectura super Ioannem], we have used the translation by James Weisheipl and Fabian Larcher: *Commentary on the Gospel of St. John,* vol. 1, trans. James A. Weisheipl, O.P., and Fabian R. Larcher, O.P. (Albany, N.Y.: Magi Books, 1980), and *Commentary on the Gospel of St. John,* vol. 2, trans. James A. Weisheipl, O.P., and Fabian R. Larcher, O.P. (Petersham, Mass.: St. Bede's Publications, 1999).

For quotations from St. Thomas's *Summa contra Gentiles,* we have used the translation by Anton Pegis et al., published by the University of Notre Dame Press in 1975.

In all cases we have sought the most literal translation, but we recognize the inadequacies of every translation, including the ones we have chosen.

FURTHER READING

Ashley, Benedict M., O.P. *Living the Truth in Love: A Biblical Introduction to Moral Theology.* New York: Alba House, 1996.

Barron, Robert. *Thomas Aquinas, Spiritual Master.* New York: Crossroad, 1996.

Burrell, David B., C.S.C. *Aquinas: God and Action.* Notre Dame, Ind.: University of Notre Dame Press, 1979

————. *Knowing the Unknowable God: Ibn-Sina, Maimonides, Aquinas.* Notre Dame, Ind.: University of Notre Dame Press, 1986.

————. *Freedom and Creation in Three Traditions.* Notre Dame, Ind.: University of Notre Dame Press, 1993.

Cessario, Romanus, O.P. *The Godly Image: Christ and Salvation in Catholic Thought from Anselm to Aquinas.* Petersham, Mass.: St. Bede's Publications, 1990.

————. *The Moral Virtues and Theological Ethics.* Notre Dame, Ind.: University of Notre Dame Press, 1991.

————. *Christian Faith and the Theological Life.* Washington, D.C.: Catholic University of America Press, 1996.

————. *Introduction to Moral Theology.* Washington, D.C.: Catholic University of America Press, 2001.

Davies, Brian, O.P. *The Thought of Thomas Aquinas.* Oxford: Clarendon Press, 1993.

Goris, Harm. *Free Creatures of an Eternal God: Thomas Aquinas on God's Infallible Foreknowledge and Irresistible Will.* Leuven: Peeters, 1996.

Hibbs, Thomas S. *Dialectic and Narrative in Aquinas.* Notre Dame, Ind.: University of Notre Dame Press, 1995.

———. *Virtue's Splendor: Wisdom, Prudence, and the Human Good.* New York: Fordham University Press, 2001.

Hill, William J., O.P. *The Three-Personed God: The Trinity as a Mystery of Salvation.* Washington, D.C.: Catholic University of America Press, 1982.

Jenkins, John I., C.S.C. *Knowledge and Faith in Thomas Aquinas.* Cambridge: Cambridge University Press, 1997.

Leget, Carlo. *Living with God: Thomas Aquinas on the Relation between Life on Earth and 'Life' after Death.* Leuven: Peeters, 1997.

Levering, Matthew. *Christ's Fulfillment of Torah and Temple: Salvation according to Thomas Aquinas.* Notre Dame, Ind.: University of Notre Dame Press, 2002.

MacIntyre, Alasdair. *Dependent Rational Animals: Why Human Beings Need the Virtues.* Chicago: Open Court, 1999.

O'Meara, Thomas F., O.P. *Thomas Aquinas, Theologian.* Notre Dame, Ind.: University of Notre Dame Press, 1997.

O'Neill, Colman E., O.P. *Sacramental Realism: A General Theory of the Sacraments.* Chicago: Midwest Theological Forum, 1998.

Pinckaers, Servais, O.P. *The Sources of Christian Ethics.* Translated by Mary Thomas Noble. Washington, D.C.: Catholic University of America Press, 1995.

Ryan, Thomas F. *Thomas Aquinas as Reader of the Psalms.* Notre Dame, Ind.: University of Notre Dame Press, 2000.

Torrell, Jean-Pierre, O.P. *Saint Thomas Aquinas.* Vol. 1, *The Person and His Work.* Translated by Robert Royal. Washington, D.C.: Catholic University of America Press, 1996.

Valkenberg, Wilhelmus. *Words of the Living God: Place and Function of Holy Scripture in the Theology of St. Thomas Aquinas.* Leuven: Peeters, 2000.

Wawrykow, Joseph. *God's Grace and Human Action: 'Merit' in the Theology of Thomas Aquinas.* Notre Dame, Ind.: University of Notre Dame Press, 1995.

Weinandy, Thomas G., O.F.M. Cap. *Does God Change?* Still River, Mass.: St. Bede's Publications, 1985.

———. *Does God Suffer?* Notre Dame, Ind.: University of Notre Dame Press, 2000.

Williams, A. N. *The Ground of Union: Deification in Aquinas and Palamas.* Oxford: Oxford University Press, 1999.

Wippel, John F. *The Metaphysical Thought of Thomas Aquinas.* Washington, D.C.: Catholic University of America Press, 2000.

INDEX

Old Law. *See* Mosaic Law
Old Testament
    Jesus Christ as prefigured in, 3
    kings in, 78
    relationship to New Testament, 3,
        66–70, 78–79, 81, 91–99, 102

Paul, St.
    on baptism, 68, 108
    on charity, 55, 68–69
    on Christ as head of Church, 108
    on Christ's death, 72
    on the Church, 73, 108
    on circumcision, 112
    on death, 40, 95, 124, 125
    on doing evil, 46
    on emotions, 48
    on end of history, 119–20
    on eternal life, 95
    on the Eucharist, 111
    on faith, 55, 68, 97
    on God's creation, 65
    on God's grace, 71
    on God's love, 18, 51, 72, 80
    on the Holy Spirit, 18, 51–52, 57, 73,
        99, 127
    on human beings as created in God's
        image, 38
    on human knowledge, 11–12
    on human merit, 72
    on humility, 80
    on the Incarnation, 18, 79
    on Jesus, 1–2, 18, 37, 40, 69, 79, 80,
        89, 95, 97
    on love of neighbor, 68–69
    on the Mosaic Law, 63–64, 67,
        68–69, 72, 97
    on original sin, 40, 92, 95
    on predestination, 36
    on resurrection of the body, 124, 125
    on saints' judgment of world, 120
    on salvation, 48, 55, 72–73, 92,
        95, 97
    on sin, 72, 101
    on theological virtues, 51

on the Trinity, 18
on the wisdom of God, 15
on the wisdom of the world, 1–2
Pelagian heresy, 72
penance, 68, 110, 115–16, 128
Percy, Walker, 3, 4
perfection
    of finite things, 10–11, 14, 28–29,
        31–32, 33, 109
    of God, 10–11, 12, 13–14, 28–29, 33,
        59, 70, 109
1 Peter
    1:18, 94
    2:5, 113
    3:21, 110
2 Peter
    1:4, 111
    1:4–5, 59
Philippians
    2:5–7, 80
    2:12–13, 48, 55
    4:4, 48
    4:6, 48
piety as gift of the Holy Spirit, 51, 54, 57
Plato, 31
prayer, 4, 55, 71, 99, 108, 109
predestination, 35–36
pride, 39, 59, 61, 80
Protestantism, 72
Proverbs 14:12, 45
providence, 32–36, 120
    as eternal law, 63–64
    relationship to free will, 34–36,
        55, 62
    relationship to predestination, 35
    relationship to sin, 41
prudence/practical wisdom, 50, 53, 54,
        56–57, 65
Psalms
    1:1–2, 44
    2:2, 78
    18:30, 14
    19:1, 32
    42:1–2, 61
    46:4, 100

CPSIA information can be obtained
at www.ICGtesting.com
Printed in the USA
LVHW111249101118
596664LV00002B/247/P